# Cartoon Monickers

Max Fleischer's Patent Drawing of the Rotoscope

# Cartoon Monickers

## An Insight Into The Animation Industry

Walter M. Brasch

Bowling Green University Popular Press
Bowling Green, Ohio 43403

to

Milton Brasch
and
Helen Haskin Brasch

# Contents

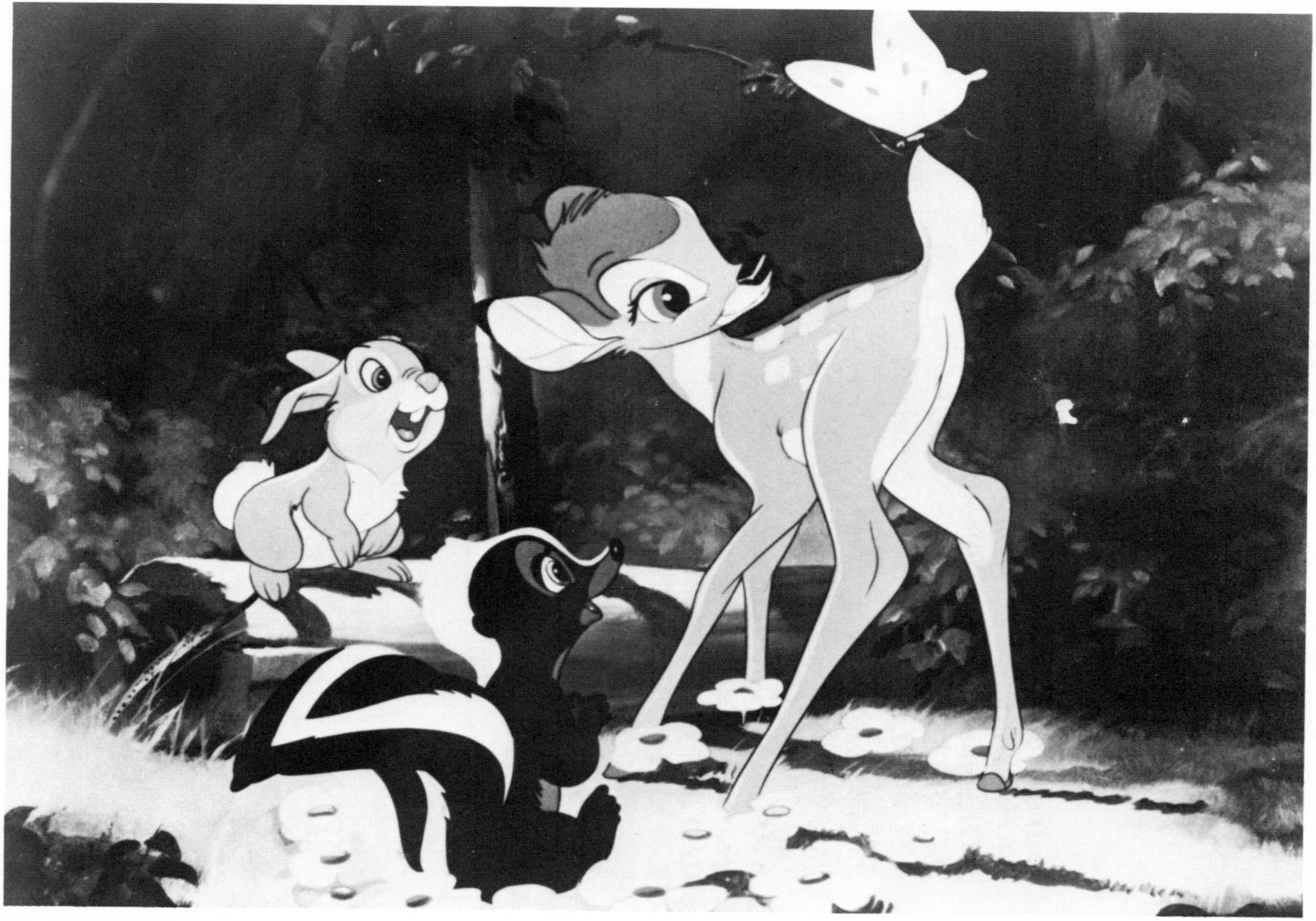

# Acknowledgements

To conduct a study of this dimension without the assistance of numerous persons in the animation industry would have been impossible. The people in the Industry—from "apprentice cel-washers" to the pioneer writers and directors—have been most helpful, generous of their time, and encouraging. Among the creative people who provided significant help are Fred ("Tex") Avery, Art Babbitt, Ralph Bakshi, Mike Barrier, Howard Beckerman, Nick Bosustow, Stephen R. Bosustow, Al Brodax, John Canemaker, Jim Carmichael, Bob Clampett, Sody Clampett, Don Crafton, Shamus Culhane, Gene Deitch, David H. DePatie, Phil Eastman, Isidore ("Friz") Freleng, Jack Hannah, Ed Hanson, Helen Hanson, Hugh Harman, T. Hee, Winston Hibler, Cal Howard, Dick Huemer, Rudy Ising, Wilfred Jackson, Chuck Jones, Mark Kausler, Isidore Klein, Walter Lantz, Jeff Lenburg, Harry Love, Mike Maltese, Leonard Maltin, Robert McKimson, Otto Messmer, Grim Natwick, Joe Oriolo, Hawley Pratt, Bill Scott, Ben Sharpsteen, Joe Simon, David Smith, Nick Tafuri, Iwao Takawara, Lloyd Turner, Jay Ward, Bill Weiss, and Jack Zander.

Bob Clampett, Chuck Jones, John Canemaker, Mike Barrier, David Smith, Joe Oriolo, and Virginia A. Duck read drafts of the manuscript and made numerous valuable suggestions which I readily acknowledge with my deep appreciation.

Most of the original art in *Cartoon Monickers* is from the personal collections of Nick Bosustow, John Canemaker, Bob Clampett, Gene Detich, Chuck Jones, and Edith Rudman of the Gallery Lainzberg (Cedar Rapids, Iowa). Studios which provided illustrations are Bosustow Productions, DePatie—Freleng Enterprises, Hanna-Barbera, King Features, Jay Ward Productions, MGM, Ralph Bakshi Productions, and Terrytoons/CBS-Viacom.

Assisting in various phases of production were Rosemary Renn Gerber and James M. Lyman. Eris-Marie Bunnell provided photographic assistance throughout the project.

From the Bowling Green University Press, I was most fortunate to have Ray and Pat Browne guide the manuscript through editing, production, promotion, and distribution. They were assisted by Becky Berry and Kathy Rogers. I am pleased to have Ray and Pat as friends as well as professional colleagues. Without their concern—which led to a major Department of Popular Culture Studies and an active publishing division—the study of popular culture in America would be severely limited.

*—Walter M. Brasch, Ph. D.*

# Introduction

Animated cartoons, whether created for the theater, commercials, classroom or television, are part of a multi-billion dollar mass communications industry that had begun shortly after the turn of the twentieth century.

For more than four decades, until the late 1960s, animated cartoons, usually five to seven minutes long, appeared with every double feature. The programs of many theaters might include the previews, one or two cartoons, a feature, one or two more cartoons, then the second feature. For only a dime in the 1920s, a quarter in the 1940s or a dollar in the 1950s, it was possible to spend an entire afternoon or evening watching twenty-four frames a second appear in continuous motion. For many, both children *and* adults, deciding which theater to go to was as simple as deciding what cartoons were being shown. And those theaters that advertised a Mickey Mouse or Bugs Bunny cartoon were often the ones that drew the large crowds. It is even reliably reported that King George V refused to watch a feature film unless it was accompanied by a Mickey Mouse cartoon.

But things changed, and for myriad reasons, most of them financial, double features were no longer part of the price of admission. And neither were cartoons. By the late 1950s, the major studios began closing their animation units. By the mid-1960s, only a few cartoons were shown in theaters; by the mid 1970s, a cartoon was a rare treat.

Television, which many have blamed for the decline of attendance at movies, was developed before World War II, but became a dominant force in mass entertainment during the 1950s. The novelty of television soon turned into the power of television. Now, instead of paying to see movies and cartoons, many people could make their own popcorn, relax in a comfortable chair, prop their feet upon a footstool, and watch half-hour shows—everything from Westerns to variety shows—for as long as they wished. All they had to do was buy the TV set; large businesses would pay for everything else.

And so to television came re-runs of theatrical cartoons. As television became even more powerful during the 1960s, studios were created solely to produce cartoons for television. Using shortcuts, such as limited animation (fewer drawings per second), the TV cartoons could be produced cheaper than theatrical cartoons. And now networks, not studios, could provide developmental money for cartoon series—the half-hour format worked quite well in television. The networks, their income dependent upon advertisers who read demographic charts and ratings analyses, could create what the advertisers wanted, who believed they knew what the public wanted. Saturday mornings became the domain of limited animation; children became the targets.

Some of the great cartoon directors went to television; most went into producing training films, or cartoons for classroom use, or television commercials; for their *own* product, advertisers wanted only the best, and directors were again given the opportunities to use full animation.

To more fully understand the animated cartoon in America, it's important to understand the historical development of the naming of animated characters. By understanding the historical trends, processes, and reasons for naming patterns, it's possible to gain a valuable insight not only into the history and nature of animated cartoons, but also into human personality as well.

*Cartoon Monickers* focuses only upon American animation, and only upon characters who either appeared in several cartoon shorts, or in major features. Nor are all characters who ever appeared on screen mentioned; rather, the study concentrates on the understanding of the nature and process of animation naming, and the establishment of a classification system. Certainly, with the proliferation of television cartoon characters in the 1970s and 1980s—many of the characters uninspired clones of comic book heroes—a full list of all characters would be impossible.

The development of character naming is not a case of spontaneous generation, with names popping in and out at the whim of their creators. It is an evolutionary process with clearly defined historical classifications. The majority of names for each historical period falls within the classification for that period. Although many names reflect earlier eras, and belong to other classifications, seldom are names reflective of classifications of future eras. The great writers and directors may not know *why* they named a particular character, and may even believe that the name "popped out of the air at a story conference," but numerous historical and subconscious patterns had already set the parameters for what the creators could say "felt good" in a name.

In the beginning years of animation, human names were combined with generic names. Mickey Mouse became the best known member of this group, but during the two decades of 1910-1930, there were hundreds of human first name/generic last name combinations, most which had a three syllable, alliterative pattern. Human descriptive names were tried for about a decade, but were soon abandoned, for the Industry was developing another class of names.

During the 1930s, descriptive-generic names began to dominate the screen. Porky Pig and Daffy Duck were two of the more famous characters.

Walt Disney's *Snow White and the Seven Dwarfs,* released in December 1937, was not only one of the most important developments in American animation, it also brought about the development of descriptive naming. The naming of the dwarfs—Bashful, Grumpy, Happy, Sleepy, Sneezy, Doc, and Dopey—led other studios to try descriptive naming.

Names already well known to the public were adapted for animated characters, beginning in the 1930s, but did not become dominant until the 1940s. The name of the Roman god of the Underworld, which was also the name for one of the planets, became the name of Mickey Mouse's dog-companion, Pluto. The sexy Betty Boop was probably based upon a characterization of vaudevillian Helen Kane who had sued Paramount, but lost when it was proven that she had based her own characterization upon another vaudevillian, Baby Esther. Others sued when they thought the characterization or name was too close to theirs, but most playfully took the similarity in stride. But the best-known name-upon-a-name was that of

Bugs Bunny who became one of animation's all-time super-stars.

Although pun-names existed since 1916, when Farmer Al Falfa was named, they didn't become prolific until after World War II. Among the better puns have been Donkey Oatie (created by Mike Maltese) and Bob Clampett's Tearalong, the Dotted Lion.

Some animators found success in *not* naming their characters, letting them become "everyman" type performers. Tex Avery's wolf, and Chuck Jones and Mike Maltese's roadrunner and coyote, were the better known no-names.

Industry-wide codes led to the absence of many possible names. But a few choice names, or phrases crept in, such as Bob Clampett having Cecil the Sea Sick Sea Serpent about to sing *Ragmop* asking for "Music, my-ass-tro, please."

During the television decades of the 1960s and 1970s, WASP names tended to dominate the television screen. The animators put the blame on the networks—"That's what the networks want. Something down the midde." The networks put the blame on the advertisers—"The advertisers don't want to upset anyone." The advertisers put the blame on the public—"Well, the viewing public, which included every race, color, and creed, didn't protest the WASP names."

As for the past and future? In names, at least, most of the characters depicted as being in the primitive past or distant future have *g* or *k* sounds in one-syllable names. Why? Probably, because, as one executive says, "It feels like it should be."

As for the cartoons themselves? The past led to a golden age in animation—full animation, expertly drawn and conceived characters, excellent scripts that kept laughter a prime ingredient. The present? Cartoon factories are churning out miles of limited animation (four frames per second instead of sixteen or twenty-four per second), designed for elementary minds on Saturday and Sunday mornings. Some series, produced by the factories, and some individual cartoons produced by the independents, are very good, perhaps even better than those from the "golden age." But, many are the equivalent of pulp fiction. The future? Why spoil it by telling you.

# Cartoon Monickers

Scooby Doo

# 1/ The Process of Naming

Fred Silverman was a happy man. It was only a few weeks before the 1969-1970 television season, and he had the confidence of a winner. From his office in "Black Rock," the CBS corporate headquarters in New York City, Fred Silverman was master of his domain. And, in 1969, his domain was daytime television for CBS.[1]

The previous year, CBS staged a coup on the other networks. It had added an hour to its Saturday morning cartoon programming. That extra hour—there would now be five hours—caught the other networks by surprise. By the time ABC and NBC cartoons hit the air at 9 a.m., CBS already had an hour jump.[2] As a result, ABC and NBC were forced to play a high-stakes "catch-up" game for the $60 million in advertising and the more than fifteen million viewers.

And now it was the Summer of 1969, a year after the CBS coup, and Fred Silverman was happy. He looked at his programming board and liked what he saw. "Penelope Pitstop will be an overnight success," he bubbled, "and after the kids see a dog named Scooby-Doo in his own series, I guarantee you there will be a million dogs named Scooby-Doo next year."[3]

There is no way to determine whether a million dogs, or *any* dogs, were named Scooby-Doo that year. But there is a way to measure the impact of Scooby-Doo on the young viewers. The dog—name and all—hit the top of the charts and stayed there. As it rose, the marketing companies realized a bonanza in sales. Soon, everything from a 3-D Scooby-Doo picture to a Scooby-Doo board game became available. By the end of 1974, Scooby-Doo items accounted for more than eighty-five percent of all items marketed in co-operation with Hanna-Barbera Productions, largest of the cartoon studios, and producers of *Scooby-Doo, Where are You?* So successful was Scooby that he later acquired a nephew, Scrappy-Doo.

Iwao Takawara, vice-president and creative director at Hanna-Barbera, gives a clue to the selling of a series to the networks. "A studio can excite a network on the basis of an idea, a name, maybe a brief characterization," says Takawara. "We ask, 'Does it interest you?' I don't think any show is sold just on the basis of a name, but the network may give us 'seed money,' developmental money, on that basis."

Inch-High, a bumbling private detective who could transform himself from man-sized to insect-sized, was first a name, then a concept. "Joe Barbera got the name," says one Hanna-Barbera executive, "then we developed the character. We sold the show to the network buyers [received developmental money] on a name and a concept."

Gene Deitch, a leading director for UPA and Terrytoons, and who later formed a highly-successful production company in Czechoslovakia, also believes in the value of the appropriate names. According to Deitch, "Aside from star names, film titles are considered as most important in selling movies. Great brain wrenching is always involved in titling movies; and in the cartoon craft, the names of the characters, especially as series headers, are our titles. It is essential to have strong, compact, memorable and evocative title names."

With such high stakes, it is reasonable to assume that extensive marketing research and pre-testing is conducted to determine the most appropriate or attention-grabbing name. However, such is usually not the case. In reality, the animation studios often play a game of onomastic roulette, picking the name that they "feel" will succeed, names that they "feel" will be acceptable to the network and advertisers. In contrast, the toy and cereal companies which sponsor the cartoons name their products only after conducting highly sophisticated research—the commercials, nine and a half minutes per hour on weekend mornings, are usually proportionately more expensive to produce than the cartoons themselves.

But in a way it's refreshing that a sense of creative "feel" is important in the development of a cartoon name. Although studios such as Hanna-Barbera now use research studies to determine *what* the public—and more specifically the networks and advertisers—want, the great directors and producers, animators and writers, the people who led animation out of its infancy and into greatness during the 1930s and 1940s, often understood the public well enough to understand human nature without resorting to "media research analysts" presenting statistical summaries on reams of paper. And for most of them, although the naming of characters could be a creative process, the most important element was the production, as the leading animator-directors worried about the quality of art, and the entertainment of the story.

Developing a name for a character, then developing a personality, is the exception in the Industry. Often, naming is an afterthought—something to worry about for functional, rather than creative reasons.

Ward Kimball, one of Walt Disney's leading animators, says, "We would have a dog in the picture. You didn't need a name because he wasn't being called. But you have to draw a model sheet for the rest of the animators because three guys might be working on it. You just can't say 'Dog' because there might be a lot of dogs. So you get a quick name. Anything that comes into your head to put on the model sheet to differentiate between other dogs that had model sheets drawn. No one ever called it that on the storyboard, and you never heard the name in the picture."

Bob McKimson, who was an animator and director for both Warner Brothers and DePatie-Freleng, pointed out that animation characters are "very seldom named before you know how they're going to act."

Writer-producer Winston Hibler who worked on several Walt Disney features, says that "We always tried to name characters according to their personalities and purpose in the story. I suppose we did, on occasion, spend a good deal of time finding a satisfactory name for a given character. But just as often, a name would pop out of the blue and everybody would say, 'That's it. Let's settle for that!'"

According to Mike Maltese, one of the Industry's leading writers, "In the pressure of time, you knock off these names. There are times that they would have been better off if they had been named something else, although I don't necessarily think that time spent on anything is going to determine whether it's good or bad. Sometimes the first spontaneous thought that you have is the best."

Jack Zander agrees. Zander, who began his career in animation in 1931 with the Harman-Ising studio, and who later headed his own studio, said, "You'd sit around the room and besides throwing darts at one another, you'd come up with names."

Kimball explains that "Of all the things I remember, the least is how and why things were named." And Maltese pointed out that "Nobody ever made an issue of it because like all history, it's not history yet. You're living it now. It's just a name and it's an everybody thing. We're making our bread and butter out of it and, we reason, 'Who cares?' You don't know how long an animation character is going to live. So you don't pay much attention to the name." And yet, animators, playing onomastic roulette, will often see their characters develop because of a name or because of audience reaction to a name. After a few cartoons in a series, the names and the characteristics are often so intertwined that it is impossible for the audience to separate the name from the personality.

Most animation characters began as secondary characters—nameless and destined to be discarded upon a pile of used cels[4]—unless rescued by the public, for it is the public that determines the longevity of any star.

Cal Howard, who entered the profession in 1930, has major credits from all the leading studios. According to Howard, one of the Industry's top storymen, "It wasn't until after they [the characters] appeared in these cartoons, and that people then liked them, that we said, 'Let's give them a meatier role. Let's build them up.' Then we *had* to give them names."

Mike Maltese noted, "There were no formal rules for naming characters. If there were rules, we would have been stifled. But, perhaps, we set up subconscious rules anyway."

Gene Deitch says that among the rules—conscious or subconscious—are "easy memorability and a clear, quick expression of character, that simultaneously sounds good and looks good in print, what is apt, and usually what seems to be funny ... not necessarily in that order of importance."

Most animators and writers agree that humor plays a large part in the naming of cartoon characters. Dick Huemer, who had a long and distinguished career with Walt Disney, noted, "We just tried to be funny. I think it was a conscious effort to be funny; to make a silly name; a ridiculous name." And Ward Kimball says, "A lot of names were picked because of their humorous sounds. There are certain words in our language that sound humorous."

Jack Hannah, a long-time Disney director, points out, "You always looked for names that would have public appeal and would seem to fit the character. Names that would be easy to say. A name that would be remembered." Stephen R. Bosustow, winner of three Academy Awards, said "I used to try to push a name that was catchy. A name that would ring . . . But that was always on the second level."

Chuck Jones, who earned three Academy Awards, and is, perhaps, best remembered for directing the Roadrunner cartoons, says that the process of naming involves a knowledge of the phonology of the language. "To me, it's a *sound* thing, not the exact wording," says Jones, explaining, "It's largely what *sounds* right in a given situation."

Other directors and producers agree. Walter Lantz, creator of Woody Woodpecker, says, "It's definitely a euphonious thing." David H. DePatie of DePatie-Freleng Enterprises, which produced the Pink Panther cartoons among other shows, also says that sound patterning has much to do with cartoon naming. "It's important that just the right sounds fit together," he says. "You have to have a *feel* for the language."

The trail from abstract "feel" to onomastic reality, while not systematic, is not as completely random as it seems to many in the Industry. The names of characters often have distinct origins and can be classified and categorized. The process of naming, and its historical development, can be described.

collection of John Canemaker

**Scene from** *Gertie the Trained Dinosaur*

# 2/ Human/Generic Naming

For three decades, people had been experimenting with full-screen animation, producing a few moments of pleasure at the most. Then, in 1906, J. Stuart Blackton, reporter-cartoonist for *The New York Evening World,* produced for American Vitagraph Studios *Humorous Phases of Funny Faces,* now regarded as the first commercial animated cartoon. The following year, Blackton directed, for Vitagraph, the stop-action animated film *L'Hotel Haunte,* the cartoon premiering in Paris. In 1908, Emile Cohl, of France, directed *Fantasmagorie,* a drama with matchstick figures; and *La Cuchemar du Fantoche* (The Puppet's Nightmare). During the next fifteen years, Cohl would direct about 250 more cartoons becoming, with Blackton, the first of the animation pioneers.

Between 1910 and 1920 the Vitagraph Studios, Ralph Barre, and Dave and Max Fleischer animated several popular newspaper comic strips, including *Little Nemo, Mutt 'n' Jeff, The Toonerville Trolley Folks, The Katzenjammer Kids, Maggie and Jiggs, Jerry on the Job, Happy Hooligan* and *Bringing Up Father,* among others.

In 1911, Winsor McCay, cartoonist for the *New York Herald,* taking a bet, created within one month four thousand separate drawings and produced the animated cartoon *Little Nemo,* based upon his newspaper series *Little Nemo in Slumberland.* McCay followed up *Little Nemo* with *How a Mosquito Operates*—the character's name was Steve Mosquito.

Although there were now many short animated cartoons being shown in the country's major cities, there were still the skeptics, those who believed that animation was nothing more than a "trick"—they believed that there were people—live human people—who manipulated the characters. The skeptics were somewhat right—animation was a trick, a very complex trick, and there were live human beings manipulating the drawings to make them move. But the skeptics were also wrong—the manipulation had been done several months before, in a studio, and not live—by trickery—at the theater, as most believed. In 1914, McCay answered the skeptics, creating an animal that no longer existed, reasoning that no one could doubt the magic of animation if he saw a non-existent animal. Standing on a vaudeville stage, McCay talked to a dinosaur, animated by ten thousand pencil drawings. He commanded her to perform tricks—some of which she at first playfully refused to perform—and even threw her an apple, which she "caught." The dinosaur, Gertie the Trained Dinosaur, established a pattern for the next fifteen years in animation character naming—a human first name and a generic last name. McCay produced eight more cartoons, including two more Gerties and a very spectacular *Sinking of the Lusitania* (1918), during the next nine years.

Among the animated characters of the early years which achieved stardom have been Bobby Bumps, created by Earl Hurd in 1915, and produced by J.R. Bray; Oswald the Rabbit (later known as Oswald the Lucky Rabbit), created by Walt Disney;[1] Flip the Frog and Willie Whopper, created by Ub Iwerks; and Toby the Pup, the lead character in a highly successful series from the Mintz studios. According to Dick Huemer, who created Toby's name, and who would later spend most of his professional career as one of Disney's top writers, "It [Toby's name] spilled out of the air. It sounded like a good name. It was a cute name. It had to be cute."

Felix the Cat, created and first animated in 1919 by Otto Messmer,[2] became an animation superstar, appearing constantly in theaters until the mid-1930s. In 1959, Felix was resurrected when Joe Oriolo created the first of 260 Felix cartoons for television. Soon, both the original Felix cartoons, and the made-for-television cartoons featuring Felix's magic bag and an evil professor, gave the black cat a new stardom. In 1982, after production had ceased several years earlier and during the time that Felix reproductions and merchandising items again became popular, Oriolo again put Felix into animation for television.

John King, producer at Paramount, the original

©1927 Pat Sullivan

Felix the Cat in *Flim Flam Films*

distribution company, is credited with naming Felix. The first two cartoons, *Feline Follies* and *Musical News* (both 1919) were so successful that Paramount decided that the cat needed a name. According to Messmer, King merged two similar Latin words—*feles* (cat) and *felix* (happy), and came up with the double-meaning Felix the Cat. At that time, the word *felix* was known by a large segment of the public as being related to felicity, happiness or good luck. Messmer also says that another reason Felix was used as a name was "because they [Paramount, the distributor] figured [that] in the stories we [needed] good luck to counteract the feeling that a black cat is bad luck."[3] Dick Huemer, one of the pioneer storymen, added another dimension to Felix's name—"Felix was probably the funniest name they could think of. There are funny names that when you are introduced to a person you have to laugh. Felix was one of these."

During the 1920s, animators began systematically dropping "the" from character names but retaining a human first name/generic last name pattern. But now, alliteration

©Ub Iwerks

Flip the Frog
A scene from *The Office Boy,* 1932

was becoming a dominant force. According to Ben Sharpsteen, a pioneer animator-director with Walt Disney for thirty years before retiring in 1959, "We thought alliteration to be an important element in the naming of our characters. In a way, it sort of added to the humor." Wilfred Jackson, who began working with Disney in 1928, and who later directed major sequences of several full-length animated features, explains another reason why the Disney people used alliteration: "Walt liked it that way. This is not only true for the names of the characters but for the names of the pictures for the most part. He liked it that way, and when Walt liked something, that's the way it was at the studio."

Disney, as well as several other producers, also favored the diminutive "-y" endings of first names. Jack Hannah, who animated and directed most of the Donald Duck cartoons for Disney, says that the "-y" ending was "to make them [the characters] seem more homey to the viewing audience. I wouldn't think of it [the name] as childish as much as I would think of it as [the audience being] familiar with it. It would seem as if you knew them for a long time."

Another part of the formula was the use of a three-syllable two-word name, again for reasons that seemed quite logical— "Walt liked it that way."

By 1928, the complete naming formula—at that time a series of rules dictated by "feel," rules usually buried in the subconscious minds of the Disney creative staff—was used for the first time on the character who was to become the all-time superstar of animation—Mickey Mouse. It was a human first name/generic last name; it had a diminutive "-y" ending on the first name; it was alliterative; and it was a three-syllable name. Mickey's girlfriend was Minnie Mouse, a name that also followed the formula, with the "-ie" ending being the female diminutive. (Interestingly, in a coincidence in which there was probably no direct relationship, Johnny Gruelle had written a series of articles about dwarfs that were published in the December 1920 to November 1921 issue of *Good Housekeeping*; one of the characters, who appeared in the March issue, was named Minnie Mouse; the dwarfs were not named.)

The embryonic Mickey Mouse was almost named Mortimer Mouse. Disney liked the name of *Mortimer Mouse*— "It has a swing," he told his wife, Lilly. According to their daughter, Diane Disney Miller, "Mother wasn't buying. She couldn't explain why the name 'Mortimer' grated; it just did." In response, Disney picked out another name with an initial -M—"How about Mickey? Mickey Mouse."[4] A name and a naming pattern were developed.

Interestingly, in 1934, six years after Mickey Mouse was named, Mickey's nephews, Ferdy and Morty Mouse, appeared in *Mickey's Steamroller*; the name Morty, the diminutive of Mortimer, followed all the rules of naming; the name Ferdy followed all rules except that of alliteration.

Mortimer Mouse finally appeared on the screen, but as a tall, lanky, rat-like figure in *Mickey's Rival*, produced in 1936. According to animator Ward Kimball, the name Mortimer was selected "to make it euphonious like Mickey. Mortimer was another name with an 'm' in it. It could have been Mustard

© Walt Disney Productions
*Mickey's Delayed Date*

Mouse or Morrie Mouse or Montgomery Mouse, but Mortimer is easier to say. A lot of [names] are chosen by the way they run off your tongue. That affected a lot of our names."

In 1931, capitalizing on Mickey Mouse's great screen success, Walt Disney, in co-operation with David McKay Co., produced *The Adventures of Mickey Mouse*. It was in that book that another character, destined to be a superstar, first appeared:

> Mickey has many friends in the old barn and the farm beside Minnie Mouse. There are Henry Horse and Carolyn Cow and Patricia Pig and Donald Duck, Clara Cluck, the Hen, Robert Rooster, all the little peep-peep chicks, and the Turkeys and Geese, too. But the Hound Dog is hardly a friend, and Claws, the Cat, is no friend at all.[5]

Three years later, the animated Donald Duck, having begun to develop his obstreperous personality, debuted in *The Wise Little Hen.*

Other Disney characters who were named on the human first name/generic last name pattern were Clarabelle Cow and Horace Horsecollar who first appeared in the 1929 cartoon *The Plow Boy;* Peter and Polly Penguin who appeared in *Peculiar Penguins* (1934); and Tillie Tiger and Elmer Elephant who appeared in *Elmer Elephant* (1936). The eight animated mice in Disney's full-length feature of *Cinderella*, released in 1950, had human first names (Gus, Jaq, Suzy, Perla, Blossom, Luke, Mert and Bert) but no last name—there would be room only for one fully-named mouse and his family in the Disney studios.

Woody Woodpecker, the red-plumed wood-boring bird that bounced onto the screen in a 1940 cartoon, *Knock, Knock,* and appeared in new episodes continually until 1972, was created and named by Walter Lantz, but originally he had a characterization not too unlike Daffy Duck's craziness. According to Lantz, his characters were usually named, "after I created the character." Woody's name follows several intertwining patterns common in the Industry—it is alliterative; it has a generic last name; and the first name combines, in one word, three separate elements—a human first name, a diminutive form of that first name, and a description of the character. Woody's name also led to some human naming. Walter Lantz proudly notes that, "We've received letters from many people who have named their children Woody." For the name of Woody's girlfriend, Lantz followed the same naming pattern to create Winnie Woodpecker. Woody's nephews, however, had descriptive names— Knothead and Splinter.

Although Walter Lantz is most closely identified with Woody Woodpecker, his studio also had a large stable of popular cartoon actors, most with human first name/generic last name combinations. In 1942 Homer Pigeon made his debut in *Pigeon Patrol.* The only other appearance was in *Pigeon-Holed* (1956). The characterization was that of Clem Kaddidlehopper, created by radio superstar Red Skelton who had expressed concern about the animated characterization.

©*Walter Lantz Productions, Inc.*

Other Lantz characters with human first name/generic last name patterns were Andy Panda who starred in twenty-seven cartoons between 1939 and 1949, Buzz Buzzard, Miranda Panda, Wally Walrus and Winchester Turtle.

Walter Lantz retained the rights to the characters he created, and was able to benefit financially from them. But the creators of animation's only ghost—namely, Casper, the Friendly Ghost—received only $175 for their apparition.

Joe Oriolo, working for the Fleisher Studio in Florida, created a friendly ghost because his daughter was afraid of ghosts, and he thought that a book about a shy, but friendly, ghost always looking for a friend might be well-received by both children and their parents. He was right. Famous Studios in New York, originally the Fleischer Studio prior to purchase by Paramount, took Oriolo's creation and Seymour Reit's story, made a number of promises—including the one that it was buying only the character and story for one cartoon, no more—and paid $175 for the rights in 1946. However, without

Oriolo's or Reit's knowledge the cartoon producer expanded it into a series, gave no on-screen credit to the creators, then sold it and all negatives, to Harvey Publications, thus effectively eliminating what would have been a series of legal actions. "My attorneys during the years," says Oriolo, "didn't pursue the matter since they reasoned that since Harvey Publications bought the character in good faith, there really wasn't much more I could do." Casper—"We were looking for a name that didn't sound as if it was very threatening"—earned the studio millions during the thirteen years he was being animated, and in the more than two decades since of television re-runs and merchandising tie-ins.

Sylvester J. Pussycat (pronounced Puttytat by Tweety Pie, the cat's prey in numerous cartoons) is Warner Brothers' only major character with a human first name/generic last name combination. Sylvester first appeared in *Life With Feathers* (1945), directed by Friz Freleng, written by Tedd Pierce and animated by Virgil Ross. In the 1947 Academy Award winning cartoon *Tweetie Pie,* also directed by Freleng, the cat was named Thomas—for Thomas (Tom) Cat.

Warner Brothers had tried using the name Sylvester once before, tagged onto a dog in a Bugs Bunny cartoon, *Hare Force* (1944), but the dog was not a continuing character. Several years later, Pierce suggested using the name Sylvester for the cat who would become the studio's best-known second banana. Freleng says that, "We thought [Sylvester] was a funny name. It was a name that no kid would like." Bob McKimson added that Sylvester was "just a name. A different kind of name. He was supposed to be an elegant bum. 'Sylvester' seemed to fit this type of character."

While Tweety Pie had his wits, and a Granny, to combat Sylvester's culinary advances, Willoughby Wren had only particles of hair, specifically, particles of Samson's hair which gave him super-bird strength when he put on a hat with those particles. The wren, under contract to Columbia Studios, starred in only three cartoons between 1943 and 1945.

In 1924, at the age of 15, Shamus Culhane had begun a

Sylvester J. Puttytat

long and distinguished career in animation. In the mid-1960s, Culhane, who had worked for most of the major studios, reached back to the adolescent age of animation naming when he named Milton the Monster. "I had a monster," says Culhane, "so I needed an alliterative first name." In an era in which naming had taken new directions, the "throw-back" to the 1920s and 1930s was unusual—and effective.

Another character with a human first name/generic last name was Fred Fallguy, created by Howard Beckerman. Fred didn't speak—his entire work day was spent rubber-stamping papers. Although he appeared in only two cartoons, Beckerman believes that Fred symbolized something important in human life—"He was a guy just trying to get by," says Beckerman, "and here was the world always falling on him."

At Terrytoons, Gene Deitch created Sick Sick Sidney, a crazy-nutty elephant who starred in nineteen cartoons between 1958 and 1963. Sick Sick Sidney, however, quickly had a name change to Silly Sidney, then to Sidney the Elephant. Bill Weiss, Terrytoon's president at the time, doesn't recall why the name Sidney was used—"I guess it just sounded good for an elephant." Also sounding good were Sidney's two companions, Stanley the Lion and Cleo the Giraffe.

In 1971, Ralph Bakshi, formerly creative director for Terrytoons, directed, from characters created by Robert Crumb, *Fritz the Cat*, the screen's first feature-length X-rated cartoon. *Fritz* quickly became a cult film, not so much for its sexually explicit scenes between consenting adult animals but because of its caustic satire of the White liberal college-age establishment, a treatment that White liberal college-age students delightfully paid for. Bakshi followed up *Fritz* with *Heavy Traffic*, *Coonskin* (1975), *Hey, Good Lookin'* (unreleased), *Wizards* (1977), *Lord of the Rings* (1978), *American Pop* (1980) and *Fire and Ice* (1983).

Among the other animated characters with human first name/generic last name combinations (and their studios) were Pete the Pup (Walter Lantz/J.R. Bray), Patty Pig, Tommy

Doggy Daddy, Yakky Doodle, Auggie Doggy

Turtle and Oliver Owl (Leon Schlesinger), Cubby Bear (Van Beuren), Felix the Fox (Paul Terry), Cecil Turtle, Charlie Dog and Henery Hawk (Warner Brothers), Clara Cluck and Humphrey the Bear (Walt Disney), Jerry Mouse, Tom Cat, and Barney Bear (MGM), Barney Barnacle and Zelda Zebra (Bob Clampett); and in a different era, for television, Luno the Flying Horse (Paul Terry), and Alan Airdale, Peter Potamus, Wally Gator, and Auggie Doggy (Hanna-Barbera). Mike Maltese, summing up the naming of a character with a human first name/generic last name, said, matter-of-factly, "They had a dog and a puppy-son. I patterned the dog father after Jimmy Durante, and called him Doggy Daddy. I called the little guy Auggie Doggy because Auggie rhymed with Doggy and it sounded good."

*Humorous Phases of Funny Faces*

Gerald McBoing Boing

# 3/ Human/Descriptive Naming

In animation, only a few characters were given human first names and descriptive last names, and even then these few characters appeared mostly in the silent cartoons during the "pre-Golden era."

For the *Chicago Herald* and the *New York Daily News*, Sidney Smith created Doc Yak. When the popularity of the comic strip was assured, Smith then put the Doc into animation in 1913. Although the six cartoons, featuring a doctor with an ability to talk into and out of adventures, was popular, the series ended in 1914.

From the J.R. Bray Studio came Bobby Bumps, Goodrich Dirt, and Judge Rummy. Bobby Bumps, directed by Earl Hurd, was one of the most popular of the silent era characters, appearing in about fifty cartoons during a four-year period beginning in 1915. Bobby, who bumped along in life, did a little of everything, and was even a war-hero during World War I.

Goodrich Dirt, directed by Wallace Carlson, also cheerfully bumped along in life; his role in that life was being a delightful and optimistic tramp. But his tramp ways ended in 1918 after two years and twenty cartoons.

Judge Rummy, created by Tad Dorgan for a newspaper comic strip, was a dog judge; but sentence was passed on the cartoons after only five episodes, all produced in 1921.

Willie Whopper was directed and produced by Ub Iwerks who had just concluded the successful Flip the Frog series. Willie, however, never came close to the popularity of Flip and was discontinued in 1934 after thirteen cartoons. Grim Natwick, one of the animators for Willie, recalls that the naming was "almost automatic." At that time, says Natwick, "a fat kid was called a whopper—'He's a real whopper!'—so I called him Whopper, then just added Willie [for alliteration]." But Willie Whopper also had a second level meaning to his

name—"A whopper is a lie," says Natwick, "and there were some un-truths about Willie."

The last major theatrical cartoon character with a human first name and a descriptive last name was Gerald McBoing Boing, one of animation's most delightful characters during the early 1950s. Theodore Geisel, writing under the name Dr. Seuss, was responsible for creating the bouncy little boy who first appeared as the title character in a short story that was later recorded. The record sold poorly, but Geisel still saw a wider audience for his creation, and went to UPA where pioneering animator-producer Stephen Bosustow worked with him. The result was an animated cartoon, directed by Robert Cannon, that won an Academy Award in 1951.

However, even with Willie Whopper in the 1930s and Gerald McBoing Boing in the 1950s, the human first name/descriptive last name pattern never did "catch on" in the Industry. It had been pleased with the human/generic pattern, and by the early 1930s was now searching for other successful patterns. The human/descriptive naming pattern was a part of that search, a forerunner that set a limited base to the next major era of naming, that of the descriptive first name/generic last name pattern.

T.S. Garp, Jr. and T.S. Garp, Sr.
Animated by John Canemaker for *The World According to Garp*

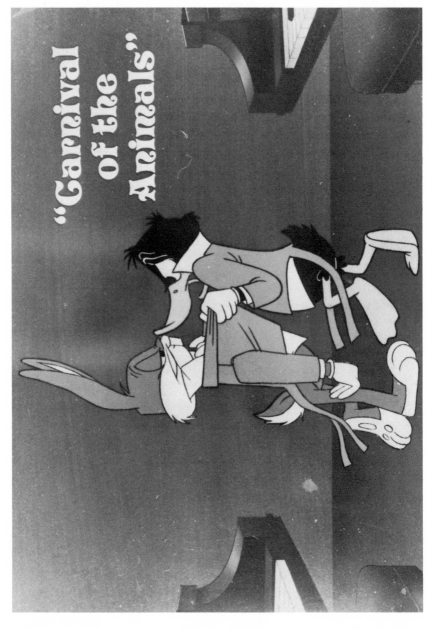

Bugs and Daffy

# 4/ Descriptive/Generic Naming

In 1910, George Herriman began drawing, for the Hearst newspapers, *The Family Upstairs,* featuring Krazy Kat, Ignatz Mouse and Offisa Bull Pupp. Six years later, Herriman, Leon Searl and Frank Moser produced the first of the Krazy Kat animated cartoons, now regarded as among the better animated cartoons of the pre-Golden Age era. Thirteen cartoons were completed in 1916 by Hearst's International Film Service before production ceased. Ten years later R-C Pictures brought Krazy Kat back for a two-year run, followed by Paramount-Famous Lasky Corporation (1927-1929), then Columbia made Krazy Kat a superstar between 1929 and 1940; most of the episodes were directed by Manny Gould and Ben Harrison. Although Krazy Kat made his animated appearance in 1916, it wasn't until the late 1920s and early 1930s that the pattern of a descriptive first name and generic last name began replacing the human first name/generic last name in popularity. And both patterns continued emphasizing alliteration or rhyming in both parts of the name.

In 1933 Walt Disney brought to the screen the allegorical fairytale of the three little pigs. The Big Bad Wolf had already been named, but for the animators, names had to be created for the pigs, even if the names were never used in the final script. According to director Wilfred Jackson, "When we talked to an animator about what he was going to do, you had to be able to indicate what character he was working on. So they [the characters] had to have names whether they appeared in the picture or whether they called each other that. This [the names] just indicated which pig [we were working on]. There was one who was practical and he built his house of bricks [Practical Pig]; one who played the fiddle [Fiddler Pig]; and one who played the pipes [Fifer Pig]." The cartoon became an animated classic, and one of the highest-grossing cartoons of all times.

For J.R. Bray, Walter Lantz created Dinky Doodle in 1924. Then in 1932, with his own studio, Lantz created Pooch the Pup and Snuffy the Skunk. Woody Woodpecker's antagonist was usually Buzz Buzzard, but in 1960 Lantz gave Woody another problem—Gabby Gator. A little more than two decades earlier, Warner Brothers also had had a Gabby, Gabby Goat, who co-starred with Porky Pig in two features, both directed by Ub Iwerks, with original concepts by Cal Howard.

At the time that Iwerks broke with Walt Disney, Hugh Harman and Rudy Ising had already left, forming their own studio, Harman-Ising. Unable to find a studio interested in distributing their cartoons, they struck a deal with Leon Schlesinger who was to become their producer. Schlesinger sold Warner Brothers on cartoons, and Warner Brothers became the distributor. In 1933, Harman and Ising went to MGM, leaving Schelsinger an independent producer with a distribution contract. Later, Warner Brothers absorbed the cartoon units.

By 1937, Warner Brothers already had its first major animated star, Porky Pig, and was looking to develop another star. The cartoon that propelled a black duck to stardom was *Porky's Duck Hunt,* directed by Tex Avery. The script called for Porky to be a hunter who was continuously outfoxed—or, rather, "outducked"—by the prey he was stalking. The original storyboard had a series of gags, each with a different duck. Bob Clampett, who was helping Avery on story and animation, says he suggested to Avery that Porky be plagued primarily by one duck instead of several, as in the original concept. In one of the first scenes, Porky confronts a little black duck who, in trying to explain that he's really harmless, says, "I'm just a crazy darn-fool duck," then swims away. Clampett says, "Tex told me, 'Make him exit funny.' So, under Tex's direction, I had him cross his eyes, do a Stan Laurel jump and some cartwheels, do a ballet pirouette, then bounce on his head and so forth."

At that time, cartoon characters didn't "go wild," and when *Porky's Duck Hunt* hit the theaters, it was, as Clampett describes, "like an explosion. People left the theaters talking about this crazy duck." The duck didn't have a name and was at first simply referred to as "the crazy darn-fool duck." But producer Leon Schlesinger was determined that the duck would be named in time for the next cartoon.

Avery said that it was a personality characteristic, a description, that was the basis for the name. He said, "Time was short, and I said, 'What the hell, we've got to call him *Duck*. So he's daffy.' It fit perfectly. There was no guesswork. No whole batch of names submitted or anything like that. I said 'Daffy Duck.' It hit me and that was it." Daffy Duck was a name that fit the character and stuck with him; the name was used for the first time in *Daffy Duck and Egghead* (1938).

Recollections vary and controversy arises as to the birth of the concept of Yosemite Sam, the sawed-off, whiskey-voiced, red-haired Bad Guy with a temper bigger than the screen, and who was Bugs Bunny's nemesis through several episodes. Participants in the idea-stage or final development of the character were Bob Clampett, Friz Freleng, Mike Maltese, and

Bob Clampett Collection

Tex Avery, with each having a slightly different recollection of the character's origin.

Clampett says that because his animated satire of *The Lone Ranger,* which he titled *The Lone Stranger and Porky,* had been so well-received by the audience five years earlier, he decided to do a second western satire, pitting Bugs against a short red-haired cowboy which he based on Red Ryder and, in part, on Red Skelton's popular western sheriff character, Sheriff Deadeye, who talked in a loud, gruff voice. In *Buckaroo Bugs* (1944), Red Hot Ryder was the good guy; Bugs was the Masked Marauder. In that cartoon, Clampett used Skelton's radio routine and had his red-haired sheriff gallop in, and then try to stop his horse by bellowing out in a loud whiskey voice, "Whoa Horse!... Whoa!... WHOA!... When I say whoa...! Aw, now, come on horse...please whoa!" The horse didn't obey any of the commands. The sheriff-like character got off the horse, ran ahead of it, then pulled a club from his pants. As the horse moved out of the scene, a large "BAM!" was heard. In later cartoons directed by Friz Freleng, there are echoes of the "Whoa Horse" bit, but with twists, as in "Whoa, Camel!" in *Sahara Hare;* and "Whoa, Dragon!" in *Knighty Knight Bugs.*

Mike Maltese disagreed that Yosemite Sam was based on the Red Skelton characterization of Sheriff Deadeye. According to Maltese, "Each animation unit at Warner Brothers had so many rabbits, so many Porkys, so many Daffys. I didn't want to use Elmer Fudd again to work with Bugs, so we drew a Western, and I dreamed up this little guy. In the pressure of time that you have, you can knock out these names. I was going to call him Texas Tiny ... Wyoming Willie ... Denver Dan. We were deliberately going for a location to make it Western. I didn't know if it was going to be worthwhile. It could have been another one-shot character. So I called him 'Yosemite Sam.' It *sounded* good to me. I had never been to Yosemite, but 'Yosemite Sam' *sounded right.* I just threw it in. Whether we used him again or not made no difference to me. I didn't care." Maltese then took his crude drawings to director Friz Freleng. According to Maltese, Freleng "resembed Yosemite Sam in temperament, and he looked somewhat like him. Of course, we had exaggerated Friz. I liked the size of Yosemite Sam. He could almost steal the picture from Bugs.

Yosemite Sam Story Sketch

His temper was larger than he was, and I played up the temper big—Sam was the Henry Hawk type—small but dangerous." The first Yosemite Sam cartoon became *Hare Trigger* (1945), written by Maltese and Tedd Pierce, and directed by Friz Freleng.

Freleng, who worked closely with Mike Maltese for several years, presents still another side of the story, clarifying some of the confusion, but giving Tex Avery the credit for originating the character that became Yosemite Sam. According to Freleng, "Indirectly, you may be affected by something that may have made you think that way. Unconsciously you may do things that you don't even know why you did it ... Maybe it was Red Skelton that was the basis for Yosemite Sam [as Clampett says]. Maybe it was me [as Maltese says]. I just draw somebody I know. I think of these characters as living characters." But the origin of Yosemite Sam was in the 1930s, not the 1940s, says Freleng. "It was an incidental character that Hawly Pratt and I designed for Tex Avery," Freleng says, explaining that "Tex had told us to make a little guy as little as his voice is big. So we did the two extremes—a big voice and a tiny guy, but he kept growing during the years because he was so tiny he couldn't work with anybody."

Another Sam—one with a similar naming pattern to Yosemite Sam—was Lariat Sam, developed at Terrytoons for the *Captain Kangaroo* series on CBS-TV. For ten years (1961-1971), Lariat Sam entertained millions of children while pursuing numerous "bad guys," including Badlands Meanie and others.

From Paul Terry, during the late 1930s, had also come Gandy Goose, an oversized baby goose who was chased by Sourpuss the Cat between 1938 and 1955, then again during the 1971-1972 television season. The goose was first named Willie Goose (both a human first name/generic last name combination and also a modestly risque pun), then renamed Gandy, apparently a reworking of gander. Interestingly, not only is gander the name for a male goose, but it also refers to a simpleton, a fool, personality traits that Gandy Goose was often accused of having. Nevertheless, because of his size, Gandy was never caught.

The year after Gandy first began bringing laughter to theater audiences, Paul Terry created Dinky Duck, his studio's answer to Walt Disney's Donald Duck and Warner Brothers' Daffy Duck. However, Dinky Duck, cute as he was, never came close to the stardom achieved by Donald or Daffy, but still starred in fifteen cartoons between 1939 and 1957. Also from Terrytoons came Deputy Dawg, a partially-stereotyped Southern sheriff who appeared in over one hundred cartoons, beginning in 1960; most of the cartoons were written by Larz Bourne. Sad Cat, created in 1965 by Ralph Bakshi, was a Cinderella-type loser, with two mean brothers; Sad Cat was not only able to survive their harassment, but also to prevail.

At MGM descriptive/generic naming was uncommon, but in 1944, Tex Avery, who had created Droopy and the wolf and was credited with having given Bugs Bunny his personality, created Screwball—Screwy for short—Squirrel. Five cartoons and two years later, MGM shelved the squirrel, one of the few times that a Tex Avery character didn't "hit" with an audience.

One cartoon superstar started out as an animated representation of a colorful flaw in a diamond, and was more popular than the live-action movie he introduced. Several film critics have suggested that the best part of Blake Edwards' 1964 mystery chase, *The Pink Panther*, was the titles. The

©Viacom

Dinky Duck

deviously humorous title section was written and directed by Friz Freleng, and featured a scrawny pink panther prancing across the screen. "The reaction to those titles was fantastic," marvels David H. DePatie of DePatie-Freleng Enterprises, "and it wasn't long before we realized we had a winner on our hands."

Within months, DePatie-Freleng began producing Pink Panther cartoons for the theater. "It was almost unbelievable," says DePatie. "Our animated Pink Panther received billing on theater marques along with the feature. Many people said they went to the feature just to see the cartoon." By the end of the 1975-1976 production season, more than a hundred Pink Panther cartoons had been produced. "A side benefit," says

DePatie, "is that the Pink Panther became a popular television series and thus extended the life of the theater shorts."

A few years after the Pink Panther became a superstar, DePatie-Freleng created another descriptive/generic character, the Blue Racer—blue for the color, racer for the kind of animal, a snake, but in true cartoon tradition, a comic snake who was forever losing his pursuit of a Japanese beetle.

Trans-Artist also had its descriptive/generic two-some, Courageous Cat and Minute Mouse who, like Snooper and Blab who preceded them, chased "evil-doers" rather than each other.

In the late 1950s, Hanna-Barbera created Huckleberry Hound, a blue-skinned bumpkin of a dog who owed his name to

©Viacom

**Mighty Mouse**

**Magilla Gorilla**

Snugglepuss

**Mr. Tweedle and Wally Gator**

**Huckleberry Hound**

a legend and a description. The legend was Mark Twain's *Huckleberry Finn.* According to a former Hanna-Barbera executive, "We named him 'Huckleberry' because ... well, it *sounded* right, and with his country bumpkin mannerisms, and his straw hat with a flower, he just seemed like a 'huckleberry'." There is no evidence that Mark Twain had the same thoughts when he named Tom Sawyer's pal, but during the intervening years, 'huckleberry' did come to have the connotation of a country bumpkin personality and gave rise to the saying, "He's just a 'huckleberry'." Hanna-Barbera later adapted Mark Twain's story of Huckleberry Finn.[1]

In 1965, Hanna-Barbera created the descriptively-named Secret Squirrel, a somewhat nutty supersleuth who spent one season fighting spies and urban criminals.

Other Hanna-Barbera characters with descriptive first names and generic last names include Atom Ant (1965-1968); Bristle Hound; Bubi Bear, from the Yiddish for "grandmother"; Doggy Daddy, Auggie Doggy's father during the 1960s; Funky Phantom, for a 1960s expression; Hokey Wolf; Lippy the Lion and his laughing hyena friend Hardy Har Har, a perpetual pessimist; Loopy de Loop, a French wolf that was Hanna-Barbera's first theatrical character (1959-1965); Magilla Gorilla, for the Yiddish word, Magilla, sarcastically meaning 'big deal'; Mildew Wolf; Morocco Mole; Motor Mouse; Mush Mouse and Punkin Puss, another cat-and-mouse team; Pooch the Pup; Ricochet Rabbit; Snagglepuss, with Daws Butler doing a Bert Lahr imitation for a cowardly lion with a touch of ham; Touche Turtle, a one-season (1962-1963) hero-turtle with a sword; and Winsome Witch, a "good" witch who used her magic in the mid-60s.

## Super People

The naming patterns of the super people are identical to the descriptive/generic naming of many animated animals—a descriptive first name and a generic last name (e.g., Plastic Man) or a combined name (e.g., Coilman). Superman, who first appeared in comic books in 1938 before being animated in 1941, was the first of the major animated super people.

Among the many other super men to appear in animated

©Viacom

Superheroes

©Jay Ward

Super Chicken

form were Aquaman, Batman, Birdman, Fluidman, Meteor Man, Mighty Man, Multaman, Plastic Man, Spiderman, Ultraman and Vapor Man.

During the early 1960s, Ralph Bakshi, who would later produce *Fritz the Cat*, the first feature-length X-rated animated cartoon, and Larz Bourne, one of the Industry's better storymen, created five wacky superpeople for Terrytoons and CBS-TV. According to Bakshi, the characters were created out of frustration and anger. Bakshi says that one of the network's top executives had come to the studio to look at proposals for Saturday morning shows, "and everything we presented, he passed on [rejected]. We gave him good stuff, and he didn't think they were right." As a joke, and with a lot of sarcasm, Bakshi, who a few months earlier had become a father, suggested that the network consider a cartoon show with a baby as a superhero. "I called him Diaper Man," says Bakshi, "and the response was unbelievable! The guy liked it! So, we just started rattling off names and characteristics." The result was not only the creation of Diaper Man, but also Tornado Man, Rope Man, Strong Man and Cuckoo Man, all of whom appeared in the same cartoons, and all of whom were semi-ordinary people who changed into their super selves when the world was in super trouble. It was the ultimate spoof of all the super heroes then proliferating in comic books and on television. For two seasons, and countless seasons of re-runs, the Five Superheroes flew across the screen saving civilization from itself.

Representing super women in animation were Spiderwoman and Wonder Woman. Adolescent super people included Bat Girl, Bird Boy, Galaxy Girl, Robin (the boy wonder who teamed with Batman), and Superboy. And, among the animals, were Manfred the Wonder Dog (with his hero-pal Tom Terrific), created by Gene Deitch and Terrytoons in 1957 for the *Captain Kangaroo* show on CBS; Terrytoons' Mighty Mouse, Underdog, with the voice of Wally Cox and produced by Leonardo Productions between 1964 and 1973; and Super Chicken. Jay Ward, creator of the super spoof chicken, reflects upon the naming and asks, "What *else* would you call a super chicken?"

Tweety Pie story sketch

Egghead
(Mid-1930s)

# 5/ Descriptive Naming

With Mickey Mouse featured in his first role in *Steamboat Willie*, released in 1928, Walt Disney had combined animation and sound. In his 1932 short, *Flowers and Trees*, Disney magic brought full-color animation to the screen. Two years later, Disney attempted the impossible—a full-length color animated feature. Winsor McCay had previously produced a full-length feature, *The Sinking of the Lusitania* (1918), and the Fleischers had produced a seven-reel scientifically-accurate, *The Einstein Theory of Relativity* (1923), but both were in black and white, both were documentaries, and only parts of the Fleischer film were animated. For the first non-documentary feature, Disney chose a Jacob Grimm fairytale about jealousy and vanity. With the screen premiere of *Snow White and the Seven Dwarfs* (December 21, 1937), a production Disney's critics had said could never be done, animation took another giant leap in both the technical and entertainment aspects of the medium. The feature had also led to the full development of descriptive naming in animation.

Descriptive/generic had been used for several years, and had served as the building blocks to the descriptive naming of the seven dwarfs. In the original Grimm fairytale, recorded about 1812, the dwarfs were not named. In the Disney adaptation, the names and characteristics would develop together.

An early version of the script named the dwarfs Blick, Flick, Glick, Snick, Plick, Whick and Quee,[2] but the final list included only descriptive names: Awful, Bashful, Biggo-Ego, Biggy, Biggy-Wiggy, Blabby, Busy, Chesty, Crabby, Cranky, Daffy, Dippy, Dirty, Dizzy, Doleful, Dumpy, Flabby, Gabby, Gaspy, Gloomy, Goopy, Graveful, Grumpy, Happy, Helpful. Hoppy, Hotsy, Hungry, Jaunty, Jumpy, Lazy, Neurtsy, Nifty, Puffy, Sappy, Scrappy, Shifty, Silly, Sleepy, Snappy, Sneezy,

Sneezy-Wheezy, Snoopy, Soulful, Strutty, Tearful, Thrifty, Weepy, Wistful and Woeful.

Five names were chosen from that original list—Bashful, Grumpy, Happy, Sleepy and Sneezy; two more—Doc and Dopey—were added later.

However, the development of the character always took precedence over the development of the name. According to Wilfred Jackson, who directed major sequences of *Snow White*, "Walt wanted to be sure we had good broad interesting personalities in the dwarfs, and they had to be something broad enough that it could come out in animation. You get a little too subtle with a personality and it does not come across with the drawings like it can with a good actor."

The naming of Doc was done after the character was developed. According to Jackson, "The guy who was aggressive and liable to take the leadership, who would say, 'We'll go this way,' so they [the other dwarfs] followed him—it wouldn't necessarily be the right way—well, what do we call him? He ended up being called 'Doc.' I suppose that would stem from the fact that a doctor is somebody who is supposed to be able to point the direction."

From throughout the Industry had come the superlatives of praise for *Snow White*, each studio eventually using some of the Disney innovation and technical advances—and descriptive naming patterns. But only one studio was willing to commit the time and resources to the production of major full-length features. The Fleischer Studio, which had recently moved from New York to Miami, created an animated version of *Gulliver's Travels*, released by Paramount in December 1939. The film shows flashes of excellence, but also looseness and haste; nevertheless, the public did accept it, though many fully recognized that no one would match Disney, not even in character development and naming patterns.

Among the *Gulliver* characters is Gabby, a dwarf-like town crier with "A real gift of gab" and a Donald Duck boisterousness in his personality. He was later to star in eight shorts in 1940 and 1941. The ruler of Lilliput was named King Little; his opponent was King Bombo of Blefusco. Bombo's spies were dwarf-like in characterization and naming—Sneak, Snoop and

©Walt Disney Productions
*Snow White and the Seven Dwarfs*

Snitch. The carrier pigeon was named Twinkletoes. The feature even had a prince and princess, Prince David and Princess Glory, whose romantic scenes—there was very little else for them to do—were somewhat like those in *Snow White*.

Other descriptive names from the Fleischer Studio were Pudgy, a mongrel; Grampy, an eccentric inventor; and Wiffle Piffle, a short-lived oddball kind of a guy with a top hat and unusual shuffle who appeared in Betty Boop cartoons. Hunky, a donkey, and her son, Spunky, appeared briefly, but never achieved success.

Goofy, Walt Disney's aptly-named human-like dog, was named the year after *Snow White* premiered, but both his characteristics and naming had been developing for six years. In 1932, Pinto Colvig, a storyman for Disney, created the voice of Goofy. Colvig had come from a small town in Oregon and, says Wilfred Jackson, "was just full of wonderful stories about

characters that he had met during his life, and incidents that happened. One of the things that he loved to do was an imitation of the village simpleton. This was just something to entertain us at the studio. This looked like a good character. The idea was that he wasn't too bright and a little happy-go-lucky." Colvig was assigned to do the voice and, says Jackson, "the search was on for a name that would suit a dog star." The first name was Dippy Dawg—Dippy being slang for someone foolish or slightly mad—and followed standard naming pattern of a descriptive first name and a generic last name. Dippy Dawg made his debut in *Mickey's Review* (1932), directed by Jackson. Later, while Disney teams were developing *Snow White*, Dippy Dawg became known as Dippy, then Dippy the Goof, the characterization having been developed by Art Babbitt. The opening line in a 1938 children's book, *Dippy the Goof*, created at Disney studios and published by the Whitman Publishing Co., was " 'Hi, Goofy!' Mickey Mouse greeted his tall friend." In 1939, Dick Huemer directed the newly-appelated Goofy in his first starring cartoon, *Goofy and Wilbur*. But the naming process didn't end there. In the 1940s and early 1950s, Goofy was also known as Mr. Geef before he was given back his name Goofy. At the studio, however, Goofy was always referred to as "The Goof."

By the end of the 1940s, descriptive naming was dominant. In the 1941 production of *Dumbo*, Disney writers named some of the elephants Prissy, Giddy, Fidgity, Giggles, Catty and Matriarch. And in *Bambi*, which premiered a year later, the skunk was named Flower; the rabbit, Thumper.

By the end of the 1940s, descriptive naming had been adopted by virtually every animation studio.

The first major Warner Brothers character with a descriptive name was Sniffles, the mouse who premiered in *Naughty But Mice,* released in May 1939. According to Chuck Jones, who directed the thirteen Sniffles cartoons, "the name [Sniffles] was not influenced by the dwarfs. He had a cold at first, hence the name."

Another descriptive-named character from Warner Brothers was Prissy, the scrawny old maid hen who co-starred with Foghorn Leghorn in cartoons during the early 1950s.

In 1943, Tex Avery, having left Warner's for MGM, created Droopy, who debuted in *Dumb-Hounded*, and starred in sixteen cartoons over the next twelve years. Avery says that he was "hunting for a character because when I went to Metro from Warner's, they said 'Give us another Bugs Bunny. That's why we got you here.' I hate to say it, but I've never come up with a character as popular as Bugs Bunny or Daffy Duck. The closest I got was Droopy." But Droopy did become a star for MGM during the 1940s. "The character came first," says Avery. "I wanted a little fellow with no reaction. I kept trying to think of new types of characters and how to handle them. There's no cartoon character that moves slow yet befuddles the villain; he's four times as small as the villain, but he outfoxes him." For his character, Avery chose a bloodhound. "A *baby* bloodhound," says Avery. "I didn't want too many wrinkles on his forehead. I didn't want him too much like a bloodhound. I wanted him on his hind legs. His name came from a droopy look on a bloodhound. It just fit the dog. He's droopy. That's the way he acts."[2]

Paramount/Famous Studios also had its dog. But this one was a news photographer (also called a news hound) chasing stories, and was not a detective/hero chasing wolves. His

©1952 MGM

name? Snapper, of course. Paramount writers, under the direction of Seymour Kneitel, also created, in 1962, the descriptively-named Swifty, a chain-smoking conman, and his mark, Shorty. Four years and twenty episodes later, they were retired.

At Terrytoons, Deputy Dawg, who had a tinge of Droopy in him, became the house dog. After Deputy Dawg came Possible Possum, a character with just the slightest tinge of Walt Kelly's Pogo.

By the end of the war, Tweety Pie emerged from the aviary to dominate the screen, the end product of several preliminary Warner's cartoons beginning in 1942.

Just as one rabbit had spawned many rabbits, and one cat-and-mouse team had spawned many cat-and-mouse teams, some studios thought that if the public liked one cat-and-canary combination, they would just love two or more cat-and-canary combinations. At the Charles Mintz Studios, the canary, a direct descendent of Flippety, a comic book bird, was the descriptively-named Flippy who was usually rescued from Flop, the cat, by Sam, the neighborhood watchdog. However, the series, begun in 1945, expired after only four cartoons.

In almost every instance, once a name was used, it stayed with the character; when the character was no longer used, neither was the name. However, there was an exception at Leon Schlesinger/Warner Brothers.

During the mid-1930s, Egghead, an oddball character whose head looked as if it could have been favorably compared to an egg, made his appearance, then starred in several cartoons. A number of persons have suggested that Egghead, based upon the characterization of comic Joe Penner, was the prototype for Elmer Fudd, but Tex Avery strongly disagreed. "No way!" says Avery. "This was just a little ad-lib guy who was funny looking. There was absolutely no resemblance to Elmer Fudd. None whatsoever!" However, in one of the ironies in animation, Egghead, in *A Feud There Was,* directed by Avery in 1938, from a story by Melvin Millar and animated by Sid Sutherland, was called "Elmer Fudd" by his motorcycle. But, the name didn't appear again until it was tagged to a new character who developed as a foil for Bugs Bunny.

In the 1940s, another Egghead appeared, this one directed

by Bob McKimson. This Egghead, however, was the superbright chicken nephew of the often-dull Foghorn Leghorn. According to McKimson, "This was about the time they were calling anyone real bright 'Egghead.' And that's why he was Egghead."

Metro-Goldwyn-Mayer also had two different characters with the same name, and even more confusing, they were both stars about the same time. Spike and Tyke were a father-and-son bulldog team, created by Bill Hanna and Joseph Barbera in 1942. The dogs appeared either as supporting players for Tom and Jerry or as stars until 1957. In 1949, Tex Avery created *his* Spike, a rather gentle bulldog who became involved in typical Avery-inspired looniness in five cartoons during the next three years.

In 1946 the Paul Terry studios created Heckle and Jeckle, a pair of talking magpies who became the first twins in animation. The names were descriptive of their personalities, and also an oblique reference to the schizophrenic Dr. Jeckle and Mr. Hyde. Bill Weiss, who was at Terrytoons at the time, and later became its president, frankly says, "I thought the names were horrible, but they stuck." In fact, they stuck so well that Heckle and Jeckle became one of the most popular characters in animation, appearing in fifty-two episodes during the next two decades.

Also from Terry came Little Roquefort, a mouse who played opposite Percy in a series of incidents not too unlike those that MGM's Tom and Jerry found themselves in. The first appearance for Roquefort and Percy was in *Cat Happy* (1950), directed by Connie Rasinski. Howard Beckerman, who worked on several of the Roquefort cartoons, recalls that the descriptive name was a part of a continuing trend. "We had the run of Something Mouse, or Something Duck, or Something Rabbit," says Beckerman, "and this had a 'nice flavor' to it, calling him a one-word descriptive name."

Other descriptive-named characters from Terry were Dingbat, Nutsy and Half-Pint, each of whom appeared only once on screen.

Some of the better examples of descriptive naming are the

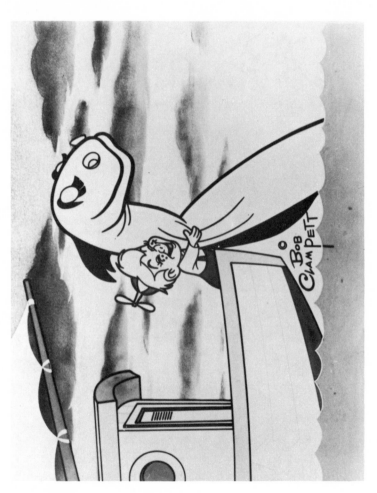

Beany and Cecil the Sea Sick Sea Serpent

Cap'n Huffenpuff, Beany, Cecil

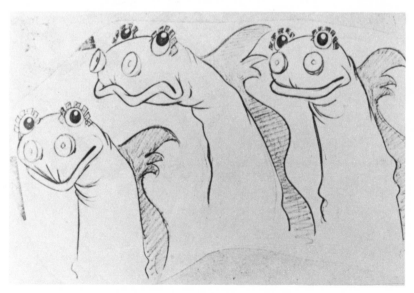

Cecil the Sea Sick Sea Serpent

Dishonest John

©Bob Clampett

monickers Bob Clampett gave key characters in his television shows, *Time for Beany, Thunderbolt the Wondercolt* and *Buffalo Billy*, among others.

The development and naming of Beany Boy, usually known as Beany, Bob Clampett's wide-eyed Innocent in a world of intrigue and adventure who had a seasick seaserpent for a friend, was the result of a lunch. According to Clampett, one day in the late 1940s, while eating lunch in Hollywood, "a very appealing little boy walked in with his mother. He had on a striped turtleneck sweater and dark overalls with straps over the shoulder, and a most winning smile. When I saw this little boy, I immediately took a paper napkin and sketched him. He had a little yarmulke which I also sketched. And then I don't quite know why, I added a propeller to the top. I knew this was 'my boy' and immediately began to think of the right name for him. When I went home that night, I wrote down a list of different names, and it struck me that because of his cap, the best one was 'Beany'." Clampett teamed Beany Boy with his Cecil and Cap'n Huffenpuff characters, then added villain Dishonest John (D.J. to his about-to-be-fleeced marks) and sold a fifteen-minute puppet series to Paramount Television, then in its infancy. The show premiered February 28, 1949. Soon the popularity spread, and *Time for Beany* became one of the nation's best-viewed shows during the 1950s. The *Saturday Evening Post* called it, "The first successful Hollywood television show," and avid fans included Albert Einstein and Groucho Marx (who called it the only children's show adult enough for his young daughter, Melinda, to watch). Clampett received three TV Academy Awards for *Time for Beany* in the 1950s. In 1959, after a decade as a puppet show, Clampett began producing *Time for Beany* cartoons; in January 1962, after several cartoons appeared in theaters, the series went to ABC-TV where it ran almost six years on prime time, then was syndicated the next eight years, topping such favorites as *Popeye, Yogi Bear* and *Tom & Jerry.*

During the early 1950s, from Cambria Productions came Clutch Cargo, an American adventurer-hero; his dachshund, Paddlefoot; and their boy-sidekick, Spinner, a boy with a Beany-like hat *and* a propeller. During the late 1950s, Stephen Bosustow's UPA produced four Ham and Hattie cartoons.

Ham—short for Hamilton Ham—was an aptly-named ham actor/musician; Hattie was a girl who wore a distinctive hat.

Also starring in only four cartoons was Windy, a country bear who was under contract to Walter Lantz studios. Director for all four cartoons was Paul J. Smith.

Walt Disney's 1959 production of *Sleeping Beauty*, written by Winston Hibler, Ed Penner and Joe Rinaldi, included several descriptive names. Among the names were Aurora, the princess, whose name was based upon the Aurora Borealis— "one of the most beautiful lights in the heavens," according to Hibler; Flora, Fauna and Merryweather, the good fairies; and the evil fairy Maleficent. Hibler, who had created the name of Maleficent from "malevolence," says that the name is just "one example of giving a name to a character's function or personality in the story."

In 1965, Nudnik, an outer space alien, made his animation debut. Gene Deitch, who directed the character in Czechoslovakia, says that the name wasn't appropriate. "A nudnik is a pest, a nag, a monumental bore," says Deitch, "but at this time, I didn't realize this at all! *My* Nudnik really should have been named 'Schlemiel' or even more, 'Schlimazl.' That's what Nudnik really was—a fellow for whom nothing went right." Deitch says that the "misnaming has saddened me over the years, for Nudnik is still a favorite character of mine." Nudnik appeared only briefly on screen, however; Deitch explains, "We started this series just as theater shorts were dying, and he never had a chance to establish himself. It was basically too expensive a series to produce to be able to convert to limited animation TV serials." Only a dozen episodes were produced between 1965 and 1967.

Prof. Kitzel starred in more than 200 five-minute educational cartoons during the late 1960s. According to Shamus Culhane, head animator for GM Productions, "In the beginning, when we were discussing these things, someone said that they were educational; I said they were not educational, just informational. I said that they should be designed to interest the child to pursue history further." Culhane notes that these cartoons were designed to "tickle" the audience—"Kitzel is the Yiddish for tickle. He became Prof. Kitzel." So, how does a man with the name Shamus Culhane

©Jay Ward

Hoppity Hooper

develop a character with a descriptive name, Kitzel? "I was raised in New York," says Culhane, "and I learned a lot of Yiddish."

From the Jay Ward studios in the 1960s came Snidely Whiplash, Dudley Do-Right's arch nemesis; and Hoppity Hooper, a lovable frog. Lloyd Turner, who wrote many of the Jay Ward scripts, says that Snidely's name "fit" the character—"He's a villain, and so is anybody that's snide. Whiplash—That's something that's going to happen to you that's not good. Snidely Whiplash was never good to you." Bill Scott, Jay Ward's chief writer, says that Hoppity Hooper was named "because we were looking for a good frog name. The first one that came to mind was Hippity Hooper. From there it was just a simple transition to make it a funnier name that sounded like a real one." Another real name was Hippety Hopper, the kangaroo that Sylvester J. Puttytat (of Tweety and

Sylvester fame) always thought was an oversized mouse.

While at MGM during the 1940s, Bill Hanna and Joe Barbera had been the creative force behind the Tom and Jerry cartoons. Now, with their own studio, one producing almost exclusively for television, they decided once again to play the cat-and-mouse game. This time they called their cat Jinks; the mouse became mice, Pixie and Dixie, all of whom starred in over fifty cartoons, beginning in 1958. Later, Hanna-Barbera teamed a cat and a mouse variation in a detective agency. The cat was descriptively named Snooper; the mouse, Blab.

In 1969, Hanna-Barbera pulled a twist in the concept of starring heroes, creating an entourage of World War I flying aces who were on the "other" side. The leader was Dastardly, his right-hand dog was Muttley; other comic flyers were the aptly-named Klunk and Zilly, none of whom could ever catch their prey, Yankee Doodle Bird, a carrier pigeon who always carried top secret messages. The gags were not too unlike those of many Roadrunner-Coyote cartoons from Warner Brothers, or ant and aardvark cartoons from DePatie-Freleng. After two years, the aces themselves were shot down. However, Muttley was resurrected in 1976-1977 season as the more descriptively-named Mumbly in his own cartoons.

Other descriptive names from Hanna-Barbera included Dingaling, a companion to Hokey Wolf; Droopalong, a companion to Richochet Rabbit; Ogee, a little girl in the *Magilla Gorilla* cartoons who always said "O gee!"; Wooly, a baby mammoth; Hoppy, a baby kangaroo; Snoots, a baby rhino; Schleprock, a teenaged walking disaster in the *Pebbles and Bamm Bamm* cartoons (1971-1976); Shaggy, a shaggy-maned teenager in the *Scooby Doo* featurettes (1969-1974, 1978-1980); Breezly, Sneezly and Sneekly in *The Adventures of Penelope Pitstop*; Botch, who had a propensity for fouling things up in *Help! It's the Hair Bear Bunch* series (1971-1972); the dog detectives Woofer and Wimper (1977-1978); and Pachy (a pachyderm) and Hoppy (a kangaroo) in the *Around the World in Eighty Days* series (1972-1973).

One character who wasn't of this world was descriptively-named Astro-Nut, an outer space character who could make himself invisible, and who comes to earth where he befriends a

Dastardly and Muttley

"timid soul," Oscar. It was the same plot of the live-action series *My Favorite Martian*, which preceded it on television by a year. The cartoons were produced by Terrytoons during the 1965-1966 television season. Hanna-Barbera later used the same idea to create Gazoo, an outer space character who frequently visited *The Flintstones*, and who could only be seen by Fred and Barney.

For decades Walt Disney had dominated feature-length productions with only the Fleischers making a serious attempt to take a share of the market. Then, in 1959, UPA brought out

*1001 Arabian Nights*, written by Dick Kinney and directed by Jack Kinney. Three years later, Chuck and Dorothy Jones wrote *Gay Purr-ee*, directed by Abe Levitow. One of the main characters was the ingeniously-descriptively-named Mewsette, a French lady cat. *Gay Purr-ee*, a delightful feature, however, was the last of UPA's feature-length productions.

The descriptively-named Blue Meanies were the antagonists of the Beatles in the psychedelically-imaginative *Yellow Submarine* (1968), directed by George Dunning, with Heinz Edelmann as chief designer, and distributed by United Artists. *Yellow Submarine* is the story of how a land—Pepperland, named for Sgt. Pepper, leader of the Lonely Hearts Club Band (which as "Sgt. Pepper's Lonely Hearts Club Band," written and recorded by the Beatles, became a musical epic)—lost its musical soul. Among the characters of the cartoons were the intellectual The Boob, Snapping Turtle Turk, Jack the Nipper, The Hidden Persuader and Old Fred, the conductor who escapes Pepperland to recruit the Beatles to journey from Liverpool to Pepperland in a yellow submarine to bring back musical life to a people who were mesmerized by the anti-music Meanies.

Among the other major animated features of the 1960s and 1970s, in addition to Ralph Bakshi's American-scene stories (see p. 19), were *A Man Called Flintstone* (directed and produced by William Hanna and Joseph Barbera, 1966); *A Boy Called Charlie Brown* (written by Charles M. Schultz, directed by Bill Melendez, produced by Melendez and Lee Mendelson, 1969); *The Phantom Tollbooth* (directed by Chuck Jones for MGM, 1971); *Charlotte's Web* (written by Earl Hammer, Jr., directed by Charles A. Nichols and Iwao Takamoto for Hanna-Barbera, 1973); *Race for Your Life, Charlie Brown* (written by Schultz, directed by Melendez, produced by Mendelson and Melendez, 1974); *Raggedy Ann and Andy* (written by Max Wiek and Patricia Thackray, from characters created by Johnny Gruelle; directed by Richard Williams, 1977); *Watership Down* (written and directed by Martin Rosen, from a story by Richard Adams, 1978); and *Bon Voyage, Charlie Brown* (written by Schultz, directed by Melendez, produced by Melendez and Mendelson, 1979).

But Disney was still the master, his studio producing,

*How the Grinch Stole Christmas*
(directed by Chuck Jones; story by Dr. Seuss)

during the 1960s, *One Hundred and One Dalmatians* (1961), *Sword in the Stone* (1963) and *The Jungle Book* (1967). In the 1970s, the studio produced *Aristocats* (1970), *Bedknobs and Broomsticks* (1971), *Robin Hood* (1973) and *The Rescuers* (1977), the last five productions directed by Wolfgang Reitherman.

Most of the characters in Disney's 1981 feature, *The Fox and the Hounds,* were named by Daniel Pratt Mannix, author of the book published in 1967. However, several incidental characters, with descriptive names, were added for the film. Among them were Dinky, a finch; Boomer, a woodpecker; and Big Mama, an owl. Ed Hanson, director of the animation unit for Disney, says that, "We were just sitting there talking, throwing around names," when Dinky and Boomer came up.

## Reduplication

A variation on the use of alliteration and rhyming in the pattern of descriptive names is the use of reduplication. In many languages reduplication is used for emphasis. In cartoon naming, it was a secondary pattern during the 1960s and 1970s, and used mostly "because it sounds good." Among the reduplicated names from Hanna-Barbera have been Bamm-Bamm, the son of Barney and Betty Rubble in *The Flintstones*; Boo Boo, Yogi Bear's cub-sized companion; Dum Dum, Touche Turtle's dog friend; Dumm Dumm and Yak Yak of *Penelope Pitstop*; and So So, the monkey companion of Peter Potamus.

## Gang Names

In literature, as in the life that serves as a base for literature, the names of gang members are usually descriptive. Hal Roach's *Our Gang* live-action comedies of the 1930s had spawned Leon Schlesinger's animated parodies. And in 1937, Walt Disney had intertwined descriptive names with a gang of seven dwarfs. However, it wasn't until 1953, with the release of Disney's *Peter Pan* that gang names again took on a major importance in animation.

The base of *Peter Pan*, James M. Barrie's brilliant story of adventure, tied together by a special magical boy who lived in Never Land and didn't want to grow up, was the tales Barrie told his children about the turn of the century. In 1901, he organized the tales into *The Boy Castaways of Black Lake Island*, more a family literary history than a novel, and placed the book on a shelf. The boys had numbers for names—No. 1, No. 2 and No. 3 (allegedly the teller of the tales); the captain was Capt. Swarthy. By 1911, however, the tales had been transformed into a play, and two gangs were dramatized. The Lost Boys were named Slightly, Tootles, Nibs, Curley, Twin 1 and Twin 2. The pirate captain was now named Capt. Hook, his personality seemingly dominated by an iron hook that replaced his right hand. His pirate crew included Cecco, Bill Jukes, Cookson, Black Murphy, Starkey, Skylights, Noodler, Mullins and Smee. For the Disney version, the Lost Boys were transformed into Foxy, Rabbit, Cubby, Skunk and the Raccoon Twins. The Pirates, however, retained the same names, with the exception that Turk was added to the group of pirates, and Cecco, Cookson and Noodles did not appear.

In the 1961 full-length Disney feature *One Hundred and One Dalmatians* the puppy game included Rolly, Patch, Penny, Lucky and Freckles. And in the 1967 adaptation of Rudyard Kipling's *Jungle Book*, Disney writers created a gang of delightful vultures—Ziggy, Buzzie, Flaps and Dizzy.

During the mid-1950s, for Warner Brothers, Friz Freleng created two gangland characters, Mugsy and Rocky, who were forever proving that crime didn't pay.

During the 1960s, Hanna-Barbera began creating animated gangs. The characterizations often bore loose similarities to the *Our Gang* comedies; the names were often hybrids between the formula of the *Our Gang* and Disney names, and the names that Arthur Laurents gave the Jets in *West Side Story*—Riff, Tony, Action, A-Rab, Baby John, Snowboy, Big Deal, Diesel, Gee-Tar, Mouthpiece and Tiger.

On *Space Kidettes* (1966-1967), the gang members are Scooter, Snoopey, Jenny Jet and Countdown. The dog is Pupstar. Just in case someone did not catch any similarities between Hanna-Barbera's cartoon series and Hal Roach's live-action series of three decades earlier, the Hanna-Barbera publicists, in one press release, referring to *Space Kidettes*, proclaimed that "Hanna-Barbera Productions presents

Heckle and Jeckle

tomorrow's 'Our Gang' of the galaxies."

In Hanna-Barbera's *Top Cat* (1961-1962), a series about cats living a New York existence, the names are Top Cat (shortened to T.C., a common identification for a gang leader), Benny, Fancy, Choo Choo, and Brain. In another feline series, *Chattanooga Cats* (1969-1971), the similarities, although less marked, are still there—Country, Scoots, Kitty-Jo and Chessie. In *The Perils of Penelope Pitstop* (1969-1970), the names for the Ant Hill Mob are Clyde, Softly, Zippy, Pockets, Dum Dum and Snoozy. The gang in *Wheelie and the Chopper Bunch* (1974-1975), are Wheelie, Chopper, Scrambles, Rota, Revs and Hi-Riser.

When the decade of the 1960s passed, there became fewer gangs; by the beginning of the 1980s, animated gangs on television, with the exception of the smurfs and other innocuous groups, was almost non-existent. But while they were on screen, they had at least one common denominator—descriptive names.

Bimbo (top) and Koko model sheet

# 6/ Names Based Upon Names

In 1922, seven years after Dave and Max Fleischer created the successful *Out of the Inkwell* series, Hugo Reisenfeld, musical director of Broadway's Rialto Theatre, and a stockholder, decided that "we've got to give him a name." The *him* was a series star, a clown who was formed out of the ink bottle, and who was drawn back into the ink bottle at the end of every cartoon, once again to become indistinguishable from the substance that created him. After discussion—some of it whether a name was needed at all—it was decided that the clown would be named Koko, after the Lord High Executioner of Gilbert and Sullivan's *Mikado*. Koko's dog, however, received the name Fido. In 1928, because of possible copyright problems, Koko was renamed Ko-Ko. Koko/Ko-Ko starred in more than one hundred cartoons in thirteen years.

In an era when animated characters either weren't named or took generic names (Gertie the Dinosaur, Kiko the Kangaroo, Puddy the Pup, Flip the Frog, Felix the Cat) Koko may well have been the first star created solely for the medium of animation named for someone else. (In 1911, George Herriman had brought Little Herman named for the Great Hermann, a magician, to the screen. But Herman had first appeared in a comic strip.)

In the mid-1920s, Walter Lantz created, for the J.R. Bray studios, cartoons featuring Dinky Doodle, a young boy, and his dog Weakheart. According to Shamus Culhane, who worked on the series, Weakheart was named "as a play upon Strong Heart," one of the leading movie dogs of the silent film era.

But the pattern of naming cartoon characters upon other names actually began about a decade later, in the 1930s, when animation entered a "second generation," one where sound merged with the visual presentation.

In 1931, Dick Huemer developed the character Scrappy, a

cute little boy. "I had a friend who had a dog named Scrappy," said Huemer, "and I thought it would be a good name to give a kid." Scrappy's dog had a descriptive name, Yippie. The extremely popular Scrappy cartoons—directed by Ub Iwerks, Sid Marcus, Art Davis and Ben Harrison, in addition to Huemer—were produced until mid-1940.

The Walt Disney animation teams often adapted well-known folklore for the screen, but seldom used the original names. According to director-producer Winston Hibler, "Unless the original story dictated strongly otherwise, we always concocted new names for our supporting characters, rather than use less interesting appelations from source materials." And seldom did any of the original characters have names based upon other names. But there were exceptions.

The farthest known planet from our sun, named for the god of the Underworld, provided the name for Mickey Mouse's dog companion. In his first cartoon, *Chain Gang*, produced in 1930, the dog was unnamed. In his second cartoon, *The Picnic* (1930), he was named Rover, an appropriate dog name, but one that wouldn't last. Ben Sharpsteen recalls, "We thought the name was too common, so we had to look for something else." Between the third cartoon, *Pioneer Days* (1930), and *The Moosehunt* (1931), Mickey's frisky friend got the basis for his permanent name. "We changed it to Pluto the Pup," says Sharpsteen, "but I don't honestly remember why." By the end of the 1930s, it was simply Pluto.

The names of two politicians and a Disney employee became the basis for the names of Donald Duck's three nephews—Huey, Dewey and Louie. One day in the late 1930s, Harry Reeves, a gagman working on the Donald Duck unit, burst into the work area of Jim Carmichael, a layout man, proclaiming, "Jim, we've got three new characters. Donald's nephews. And we're gonna work them into a lot of screwy situations with the duck. But we haven't got names for 'em. Got any ideas for naming three cute lit'l ducks?"

Carmichael recalls that he "wasn't too interested that morning in the nomenclature of three cute li'l ducks, so I glanced at the front page of the newspaper." According to Carmichael, "Thomas E. Dewey was doing something political in New York, and Huey P. Long was blabbering in New

Donald Duck and Nephews

Orleans. So, off-handedly, I said, 'Why don't you call them Huey and Dewey?' A friend of mine, Louie Schmitt, was passing in the hall and gave the big hello. Inspired, I said, 'Hell, call the little clunkers Huey, Dewey and Louie.' Harry leaped up, yelping, 'That's IT ... Oh boy! ... Huey, Dewey and Louie! Perfect!' He dashed from the room and that, odd as it may sound, was how the three ducks got christened. At the time I thought it might have been just another gag—Walt's pixies were always playing them on each other—but, lo and behold, the next Duck epic had three little tykes in it, all properly appelated." (The nephews' mother—there was no mention of a father—was named Sister Dumbella, a descriptive name.)

Although Donald's nephews were named for people, Daisy's nieces were named for months—April, May and June—although their names appeared only in comic books.

Other Disney ducks, both related to Donald Duck, also owed their names to someone else. During many of the "space race" years after Sputnik, rocket scientist Wernher Von Braun was a consultant to the Disney studios. In 1961 Von Braun was loosely transformed into animation as scientist Ludwig Von Drake, and made his first appearance in *Scrooge McDuck and Money,* a segment for television. And in 1967, Scrooge McDuck, whose name and miserly character was based upon Charles Dickens' villain of *A Christmas Carol*, was introduced on screen as Donald Duck's uncle. After several years as a comic book character, in December 1982, Scrooge returned to the screen in the role of his namesake in a 30-minute featurette based upon the Dickens story. Also appearing were all the continuing Disney characters in their first return to the screen in over a decade.

Other exceptions in the name-on-name restrictions were in *Dumbo*, the animated feature with a circus setting about a little elephant with big ears and an even bigger heart.[1] Helen Aberson and Harold Pearl had written the story; Walt Disney selected Dick Huemer and Joe Grant to adapt it for the screen. And so Huemer and Grant put their creative minds to work to develop Disney's fourth animated feature, released in late 1941. The matriarch of the elephants was named Mrs. Jumbo. Huemer explains that "We were thinking of the P.T. Barnum elephant [of the 1880s]. That's the most famous elephant there ever was." (An incidental character in Winsor McCay's *Gertie* was a baby wooly mammoth named Jumbo.) The elephant trainer in *Dumbo* was named Joe; but, Huemer says that the character wasn't named after anyone—"Joe was just a name. The first name that came to us." The anthropomorphized circus train, however, was proudly named Casey Jones—"a tribute to the great engineer."

One of the outstanding segments of *Dumbo* was the crows sequence, brilliantly and imaginatively animated by Ward Kimball. One of the crows was named Jim Crow, but none of the other crows had on-screen names.

Mason Locke Weems, better known as Parson Weems, an early nineteenth century American writer and bookseller, found his name remotely appropriated by Disney writers who created super genius Baby Weems, title character in a segment of *The Reluctant Dragon* feature (1941). Writer-animator Dick Huemer said he didn't remember why the name Weems was used—"I guess it just sounded right."

In 1946 Walt Disney immortalized Gatty Kazaza as Tetti Tatti. Kazaza had run the Metropolitan Opera during Caruso's greatest years; Tatti ran the Met during the time that Willie the Whale wanted to become an opera star in the delightful cartoon featurette *The Whale Who Wanted to Sing at the Met,* a part of Disney's full-length feature *Make Mine Music.* But, animators weren't finished with Gatty Kazaza's name. In 1964, Chuck Jones and Mike Maltese, working for MGM, cast Tom (in a Tom and Jerry cat-and-mouse cartoon) as opera star Thomassina Catti-Cazzaza in *The Cat Above and the Mouse Below.*

Winnifred Hannah, the wife of director Jack Hannah, was indirectly responsible for the naming of the one-appearance delightful character Bootle Beetle, a meek and trusting little beetle who appeared as the title character in a 1947 Disney cartoon. According to Hannah, his wife had mentioned that there was a horse, Beetle Bootle, running at the Pomona Fairgrounds—"so I traversed it and named him Bootle Beetle."

In 1943, two mischievous chipmunks, playful antagonists for Donald Duck, made their debut in *Private Pluto.* According to Jack Hannah who directed most of the Donald Duck cartoons for the Disney studio, "At first, they were just foils for the duck. But they became an immediate hit, and we decided they were strong enough to give them names." And so, one day in 1947, with Jack Hannah and several assistants in Hannah's office, names were created for the chipmunks. Hannah recalls, "There were four or five of us in my office, and Bea Selck, my assistant director, happened to pipe out the name Chippendale because of the furniture designed in the eighteenth century by Thomas Chippendale. Immediately, I said, 'That's it! That's their names!' She just threw it out in the meeting and I jumped on it as being the name that fit them just right." Thus the two previously unnamed chipmunks, now stars on their own, were named Chip an' Dale.

The splitting of names continued in animation when Mike Sasanoff and Bob Clampett in 1947, following similar linguistic naming rules, split the Scottish name, MacIntosh, into Mac 'n' Tosh for two equally delightful and very deferential gophers. The characterization was based upon F. Opper's comic strip team Alphonse and Gaston, whose running gag was to be overly polite to each other. (McIntosh was the name of a popular clothing store on Hollywood Blvd. where some staff members bought their clothes.) Two not-so-polite characters, however, were Si and Am, Siamese cats created in 1955 by Disney for his full-length feature *The Lady and the Tramp.*

Although other studios used in-house naming gags—character names based upon the names of the creative staff—there were relatively few in-house gags at the Disney studios. Nevertheless, in five cartoons—*Ferdinand the Bull* (1938), *The Nifty Nineties* (1940), *Hockey Homicide* (1945), *Duck Pimples* (1945) and *Double Dribble* (1946)—Disney writers and animators found themselves caricatured and/or named, the only on-screen tributes to some of the most creative people in the Industry.

In the early 1930s, the Van Beuren Studio, a small animation studio which was to produce popular cartoons but have a short life, created two little-remembered Mutt 'n' Jeff-like characters who appeared in twenty-six cartoons. Tom was a big man; Jerry was a small man. The name origin was from Pierce Egan's 1821 book, published in London, *Life in London:*

Tom and Jerry

Pixie, Dixie, Jinx

*Or, the Day and Night Scenes of Jerry Hawthorne, esq., and His Elegant Friend, Corinthian Tom.*

In 1940, four years after Van Beuren ended production, Rudy Ising produced, for MGM, *Puss Gets the Boot*. The cat was named Jasper; the mouse had no name. When *Puss Gets the Boot* received an extremely favorable reaction in the theaters, MGM decided to feature the cat and mouse in other episodes, but were stymied for permanent names. Joe Barbera, who had been a story man for the Tom and Jerry cartoons at Van Beuren, and who, with Bill Hanna directed *Puss Gets the Boot*—suggested that the MGM cat be named Tom (the usual pun, Tom Cat), and the MGM mouse be named Jerry. The names stuck, and Tom and Jerry became MGM's first animated superstars, earning seven Academy Awards.

Later in the decade, Official Films, a home movie distributor, bought the rights to the Van Beuren films, but because of the popularity of the cat-and-mouse Tom and Jerry, had to rename the original characters. Tom became Dick; Jerry became Larry. Even Cubby Bear, a popular bear cub, was renamed, becoming known as Brownie.


For some time, Paramount executives had thought of dropping *Little Lulu*, one of its most successful series. *Little Lulu* was making money, but not enough money; all the non-animation rights were owned by Marjorie Henderson Buell who had created the character which still appeared regularly in the *Saturday Evening Post*. Then, in mid-1948, Little Audrey, originally a comic book character, was born into animation, and Little Lulu, who starred from 1944 to 1948, was shelved.

Howard Beckerman, who worked for Terrytoons which produced Little Lulu and then Little Audrey for distribution by Paramount, says a couple of factors entered into the naming of Little Audrey. "It sounded like Little Lulu," he notes, "and during the 1920s and 1930s, when most of the animators were children, there were little Audrey jokes; these were quite similar to the "Little Moron" jokes. Little Audrey, however, never reached the fame of her predecessor, and starred in only thirteen cartoons during the next eleven years although she was directed by Seymour Kneitel, Isadore Sparber and Bill Tytla, among the best in the Industry.

Other "little" characters, none of whom reached stardom, were Li'l Abner (Columbia, 1944-1945), based upon the Al Capp comic strip; Little Herman (1911), based upon the George Herriman comic strip; Little Iodine, based upon the Jimmy Hatlo comic strip; the Little King (Van Beuren, 1933-1934), based upon the Otto Soglow comic strip; and Little Roquefort (Terrytoons, 1950-1955).

When Hugh Harman and Rudy Ising split from Leon Schlesinger in 1933, they took with them Bosko, the studio's only cartoon star. This left Schlesinger with only the titles Looney Tunes and Merrie Melodies. To compensate for the loss, Schlesinger introduced a new lead character into Looney Tunes named Buddy, created by gag-man Earl Duvall. Buddy, essentially a clone of Bosko, was proving to be a disappointment, and a better character was urgently needed.

Schlesinger suggested to the staff that if they couldn't think of one good character, they could perhaps come up with a group of characters, an animal version of Hal Roach's *Our Gang* comedies. In one of the idea meetings, it was brought up that the *Our Gang* shorts always had an appealing little fat boy and a cute black youngster named after something to eat— "Farina" (a breakfast cereal) and later "Buckwheat."

According to Bob Clampett, "Someone thought of two puppies named Ham and Ex, and that started me thinking. So after dinner one night, I came up with Porky and Beans. I made a drawing of this fat little pig, which I named Porky, and a little Black cat named Beans. Under the drawing, in imitation of the lettering on a can of Campbell's Pork and Beans, I wrote 'Clampett's Porky and Beans', and showed it to Leon [Scheslinger]" who later noted "The boys and I went into a huddle and came out with six new characters for *I Haven't Got a Hat.* (Porky, Beans, Ham, Ex, Oliver Owl and Kitty Kat.)

Schlesinger then hired Joe Dougherty, a Warner contract actor friend who actually stuttered, to do Porky's voice.[2] Schlesinger's gang made their debut in *I Haven't Got a Hat* (1935), under the direction of Friz Freleng, with Porky's key stuttering scene animated by Bob McKimson.

**Porky Pig**

**Main Title Card (1935)**

Elmer Fudd model sketch

The immediate success of the new characters prompted Schlesinger to have the "Looney Tunes" main title redesigned replacing the likeness of Buddy with that of "Gang" members Porky, Beans, Kitty and Oliver Owl. Jack King directed nearly a dozen Looney Tunes featuring Beans and/or Porky, before returning to the Disney Studio where he directed Donald Duck shorts. When Tex Avery joined the Schlesinger organization, his first cartoon was *Gold Diggers of '49* (released January 6, 1936), featuring gang members animated by Bob Clampett and Chuck Jones. Porky appeared in almost two hundred cartoons in a three-decade career that didn't end until 1965.

Porky's girlfriend, developed by Frank Tashlin and Clampett, was named Petunia Pig, her name following the general rule patterns as those that created Porky Pig's name—Porky's was alliterative and, at the same time, both descriptive/generic and a name based upon a name; Petunia's name was also alliterative, descriptive/generic (cute like a flower), and a name based upon a name, only in this case a flower not a person.

Tex Avery coined the name for Elmer Fudd who was to become Bugs Bunny's nemesis in numerous cartoons. The name was based upon the reworking of a song lyric of *Mississippi Mud*, an early 1920s hit. One of the lines was, "It's a treat to beat you on the Mississippi mud—Uncle Fudd," with the "Uncle Fudd" often stretched out. "So, in school," said Avery, "we used to call him Uncle Fudd and get a big laugh. It stuck with me, so we stuck it as Elmer Fudd." The name first appeared on the screen in *A Feud There Was* (1938), directed by Avery.

In 1946, while at MGM, Avery created, from a story by Heck Allen, *Lonesome Lenny*, a parody of John Steinbeck's *Of Mice and Men*. Lenny, a dog as strong and kind as he was dim-witted, became Screwy Squirrel's companion for one cartoon in 1946. The popularity of the cartoon led Avery to create two permanent bear-like characters, George and Junior, who starred in *Henpecked Hoboes* (1946), *Hound Hunters* and *Red Hot Rangers* (both 1947) and *Half-Pint Pygmy* (1948).

Even *Uncle Tom's Cabin*, Harriet Beecher Stowe's powerful abolitionist story, was not safe from Avery's wild satire. In 1937, while working for Leon Schlesinger, Avery created *Uncle Tom's Bungalow,* a not-too-successful spoof, animated by Virgil Ross and Sid Sutherland. Then in 1947 Avery directed, for MGM, *Uncle Tom's Cabana,* from a story by Heck Allen, with animation by Ray Abrams, Robert Bentley, Preston Blair and Walter Clinton. *Uncle Tom's Cabana,* which became one of Avery's finest cartoons, focused upon the villainous Simon Legree who owns everything in a metropolitan concrete city but the small log cabin of Uncle Tom who now faced foreclosure.

### All About Rabbits

Oswald the Lucky Rabbit was probably the first rabbit to achieve stardom, first in the 1920s for Walt Disney who created him, then for Walter Lantz who acquired the rights.

In 1934, Wilfred Jackson directed *The Tortoise and the Hare,* the Walt Disney version of Aesop's fable; the cartoon earned an Academy Award. The tortoise had a human/generic name, Toby Tortoise. The hare, the cocky speedster who runs circles around the tortoise only to lose at the finish line, was named Max Hare, a take-off on the name of boxer Max Baer. The following year, Disney brought out a sequel, *Toby Tortoise Returns,* and both the tortoise and the hare achieved a brief stardom.

In 1931, Bob Clampett had created a "wabbit" for a possible cartoon subject. He recalls that one day, while working at Harman-Ising studios, Rudy Ising, in all seriousness, told everyone about the frustrating time he had trying to hunt a rabbit. Every time Ising had the rabbit almost in his sights, the rabbit would disappear, only to pop up somewhere else. Clampett says, "We thought it was hilarious and began drawing caricatures of Rudy in a hunter's outfit trying to track down an elusive rabbit. On one of the drawings, I changed the original inscription of 'Rudy Rabbit' to 'Wudy Wabbit.'" Clampett says he then drew a series of gags showing the "wabbit" character outwitting the hunter, and submitted them as a possible cartoon subject. However, the idea died.

Later, when Leon Schlesinger needed a story, he asked Clampett if he had any simple two- or three-character story ideas that could go into production quickly. Clampett suggested that he could take the leftover gags that weren't used in *Porky's Duck Hunt* (directed by Tex Avery, and animated by Clampett), add new material, and have a story ready in a few days. Although Schlesinger didn't object to a hunting story, he did object to another duck hunt. (*Porky's Duck Hunt* had introduced the character who would become Daffy Duck.) Remembering his Wudy Wabbit idea several years earlier, Clampett decided that his prey should be a rabbit. He then drew up a series of gags, which Schlesinger approved. *Porky's Hare Hunt,* directed by Ben Hardaway, included the gags of a rabbit doing a fake dying scene, munching on a carrot, doing a magical "hare remover" bit, proclaiming, "Of *course,* you know this means war!" and marching off stiff-legged, playing an imaginary fife. When the cartoon received favorable comment from the theater managers, Warner Brothers decided to go with another rabbit hunt. Hardaway and Dalton then directed, from a story by Tubby Millar, *Hare-um Scare-um* (1939). Clampett's suggestion of changing the "r" sounds to "w" sounds led to dialogue that included, "wittle gwey wabbit" and "wabbit twaks," all spoken by Elmer Fudd. Then, from a story by Rich Hogan, Chuck Jones directed *Elmer's Candid Camera* (1940) which featured another version of the rabbit. And Elmer, dressed in his customary derby, high collar, and coat said "wabbit" on the screen for the first time, and also talked about a "wittle gwey wabbit" and "wabbit twaks." It was the third major Warner's cartoon to feature a rabbit hunt, and each rabbit had a slightly different personality. (Elmer Fudd, with his new speech pattern, next starred in two rabbit-less cartoons, *Confederate Honey* and *The Hardship of Miles Standish,* both directed in 1940 by Friz Freleng.)

Then, later in 1940, Tex Avery combined Elmer Fudd, now dressed in a hunter's outfit, and a rabbit, in *A Wild Hare*; the story was written by Rich Hogan; Virgil Ross was the animator. This "wild hare" was different from the other three; it was a more lanky, aggressive rabbit, one with a superior intellect and wit. And Mel Blanc gave it the voice of a Brooklyn street-wise rabbit. The story reprised the best ideas from the three previous rabbit cartoons, including the fake dying act, the rabbit putting his hands over the hunter's eyes and asking, "Guess Who?" the omnipresent carrot (which became a

Lil' Wuddy Wabbit

modified flute), and the hunter spotting "wabbit twaks."

Avery noted that "We thought it was just another character. It got laughs. But not much was thought of it. It was just another rabbit." Within days of its release, however, exhibitors began writing to Jack Warner to tell him how popular the rabbit was with the audiences. Within weeks, *A Wild Hare* became one of the most popular cartoons ever produced, and Warner told producer Leon Schlesinger to begin making "more rabbit pictures." According to Avery, until Warner made the decision to feature the rabbit, there was no discussion as to name—"one-time" characters usually didn't have on-screen names. But now that Jack Warner himself was backing the rabbit—well, that was a different matter—after all, you can't have a star without a name. Thus, says Avery, began one of the greatest name hunts in animation. Avery made his pitch to call the rabbit Jack E. Rabbit because he had shot jack rabbits in Texas as a kid, and because, "I thought it would please my Texas friends." Clampett and Tedd Pierce suggested Bugsy Rabbit, for mobster Bugsy Siegel. Numerous suggestions were made using the pattern of a human first name and the generic last name of Rabbit. Other names stressed a descriptive first name and generic last name, by now a common pattern.

The previous year, in one of the interesting coincidences in animation, a name had been "tagged" onto a rabbit—not Avery's "wild hare," but the rabbit of Hardaway's *Hare-um Scare-um*. Hardaway, known as Bugs, had sent preliminary sketches of the rabbit to illustrator Charles Thorson for additional work. Thorson took the idea, prepared several sketches, and then sent the revised drawings back to Hardaway. To identify the sketches, Thorson noted that they were "Bugs' bunny."

Then, with the success of the fourth rabbit picture, when everyone was desperately searching for an on-screen name, "Bugs Bunny" (without the possessive form) came up. Publicist Rose Hoarsley liked the name. According to Avery, she said it was "so cute. And Bugs Hardaway does work here. We'll play it two ways!" But Avery said he disagreed—*strongly*. "Mine's a *rabbit!*" he protested. "A tall, lanky, mean rabbit. He isn't a fuzzy little bunny." He said that "Bugs

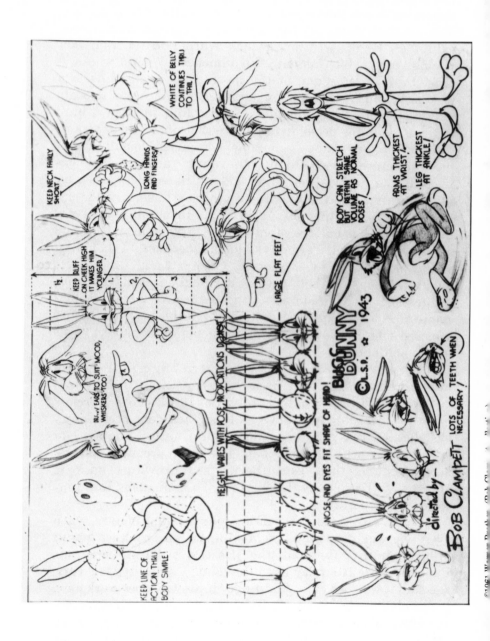

Bunny" sounded too much like a Walt Disney character. But the publicist persisted, and Avery didn't fight it too hard. She took the name to Producer Leon Schlesinger. Schlesinger, says Avery, "wasn't great on entering into anything [we created] as long as it was a funny character [and in good taste]. Schlesinger thought a moment, then said, 'O.K. Bugs Bunny. We'll go with it'." In 1945, Bugs Bunny was voted the animated box office champion. After Bugs Bunny achieved stardom, numerous persons—writers and reporters, those in the animation industry and those who just came to theaters and enjoyed the cartoons—began searching for Bugs' roots. Many claimed that Bugs first appeared in *Hare-Um Scare-um; others* saw the origin of Bugs in other rabbits, especially in the Wudy Wabbit of Bob Clampett and in *Porky's Hare Hunt*. It wasn't too long before numerous people—some with legitimate claims, some with publicity-seeking egos—began claiming a part in Bugs' creation. Even the name was never settled, as numerous persons—including Mel Blanc, the voice of numerous cartoon stars, including Bugs—claimed either a part or the entire credit for the name, although most of them acknowledged that the "Bugs" of Bugs Bunny was based upon "Bugs" Hardaway's nickname. The question over who created the character Bugs Bunny probably will never be decided, the truth lost in the catacombs of history.

But in another one of those ironies of creation, ask any Disney veteran who created Bugs, and you get an opinion that it is likely that Tex Avery was responsible for the character that became Bugs, but that Bugs was based upon another character—one created by Disney. Director Jack Hannah says that "Bugs Bunny was a direct takeoff on that cocky rabbit [in *The Tortoise and the Hare*], and yet I can't say Bugs Bunny was born because of that rabbit." Director-producer Wilfred Jackson goes a little further, noting that Bugs Bunny as a character was simply lifted out of *Tortoise and the Hare*. There was no trouble about copyright, but we had a definite feeling that the character was lifted out of ours. Those of us who worked on the picture were a little indignant at the similarity. There was a little bit of feeling that someone ought to do something about it." Even Tex Avery acknowledged his debt to Disney. "As a drawing," said Avery, "Bugs Bunny has an

Tortoise and Hare

awful lot in common with Max Hare ... but Mr. Disney was polite enough never to mention it, because he didn't have to. People had been copying him for years, his bears and everything else, but he never did complain. He evidently looked at us as parasites."[3] (Even Disney's series titles were appropriated. Silly Symphonies was the series title Disney gave to several cartoons which featured a musical score intertwined with the animation. Schlesinger/Warner Brothers liked the idea so much that it developed two series, Merrie Melodies and Loony Tunes. MGM, a few years later, created Happy Harmonies.)

In 1941, Avery directed the Leon Schlesinger/Warner Brothers version, *Tortoise wins by a Hare,* written by David Monohan, and animated by Charles McKimson. According to Avery, "... If you look back, there's a rabbit that looked a heck of a lot like Bugs Bunny, as far as the drawing goes. But he wasn't Bugs Bunny without the gags we gave him."[4] And few will argue that it was Tex Avery who gave his particular rabbit a special vitality to become the wise-cracking superstar he became. And, further, no one will deny that after Avery moved to MGM,[5] the direction of Bob Clampett, Chuck Jones, Friz Freleng and Bob McKimson kept the rabbit a superstar for more than four decades.

Walt Disney and Warner Brothers weren't the only studios to pull rabbits out of their drawing boards. Soon, rabbits began multiplying, keeping writers and animators busy during the 1940s. Then, in the early 1950s, Harvey Films created a rabbit-turtle combination. The turtle was Tommy Tortoise—his name following the pattern established in the 1920s; the rabbit was Moe Hare, a pun as well as a human first name/generic last name pattern and, quite possibly, a similarity to Disney's Max Hare. The rabbit was a city-slick conman; the turtle was the prey. And, as might be expected, one of the cartoons in the series was a story of how the turtle—now aided by a jet pack—defeats the rabbit. Just as audiences loved the other turtle-rabbit chases, so they also loved this one, directed by I. Sparber, and it is doubtful that anyone complained that it was "just another chase."

Several years later, Hanna-Barbera created Ricochet

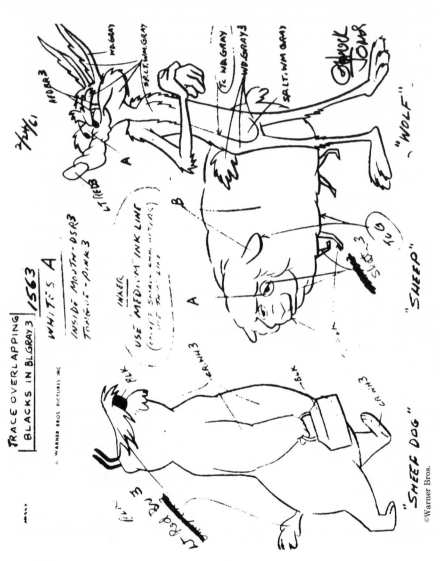

©Warner Bros.

Model Sheet for Sam Sheep Dog and Ralph Wolf

Rabbit, a cock-sure sheriff in an "Old West" setting. During the 1960s, Warner Brothers added three more quickly-forgotten rabbits to animation history—Bunny and Claude, based upon the popular movie *Bonnie and Clyde*; and Rapid Rabbit.

## In-House Naming

The naming of Bugs Bunny for Bugs Hardaway was the most popularized "inside" naming at Warner Brothers. But there were others. Mike Maltese participated in the naming of Hubie and Bertie, two "very British" mice who appeared in three cartoons. Hubie was named after Hubie Karp, one of the industry's leading storymen. As for the naming of Bertie, Maltese says, "We just threw it in. It was the name that first came to our minds; it just sounded right with Hubie."

Maltese, himself, was "immortalized" in celluloid as the S.S. Mike Maltese, a ship that carried a small pink elephant to New York in *Punch Trunk*, directed by Chuck Jones. Jones received some additional onscreen credit in two of his somewhat wacky Bugs Bunny tributes to opera. In *What's Opera, Doc?* the star was Giovanni Jones; in *The Rabbit of Seville* (1950), Carlo Jonsi was given a credit in the opera-within-a-cartoon. And Bob McKimson gleefully recalled that, "There are many, many McKimson Buildings in Warner Brothers cartoons."

A Warner Brothers creation, with names similar to the early cartoon names, was the series featuring Sam Sheepdog and Ralph Wolf, developed about 1952. For an eight-hour work day—plus lunch breaks—the wolf would deviously try to capture the sheepdog's sheep, only to be continuously frustrated. "It just sounded like it should be *Sam* for the sheepdog," says director Chuck Jones. "But as for Ralph ... Well, there was a cartoonist named Ralph Wolf and I always wanted to use the name." If pronounced as intended, there is also an ominous sound to the name of the sheep-stealing Ralph Wolf.

A writer may have unwittingly contributed his own name to Ralph Wolf, but an orator-dictator, long dead, was resurrected by Jones and by Mike Maltese as a fierce bulldog with a large heart. Marc Antony starred in a few excellent

Mister Magoo

cartoons beginning with *Feed the Kitty* (1952), but never achieved the stardom hoped for by studio executives.

Chuck Jones also directed, from a script by Mike Maltese, Michigan J. Frog's debut in *One Froggy Evening*, produced in 1956. In this classic, a construction worker finds a vaudevillian frog, one who sings and dances. But the frog will perform only for his discoverer. Jones says that he chose the name "because the frog sang *The Michigan Rag* [a song composed for the cartoon], and it only seemed appropriate."

Mr. Magoo, the bumbling near-sighted but lovable character from UPA, was developed by Millard Kaufman under the direction of John Hubley and Stephen Bosustow. Later, Pete Burness directed most of the Magoos. According to Bosustow, whose studio earned two Academy Awards for Magoo cartoons, the name was appropriated from a character in a Broadway play. Phil Eastman, who worked on many of the Magoo cartoons, remembers that Hubley "was fascinated by that name. It's a funny name." "The Magoo character," explained Bosustow, "epitomized what everybody wanted to do. People would like to accomplish things by luck, by chance, by circumstances, but without working for it. They would like to think they could do it—to have the thought and then it would happen."

In his fifty-two episodes, Magoo didn't have a first name— "We tried to dream one up but never did; none seemed to fit," says Bosustow. When Magoo underwent a resurrection on television several years later, he was tagged with a seldom-used name of Quincy.

But Bosustow said that he seldom created animated names based upon other names for characters in the many educational cartoons he produced. He said, "The story is the thing . . . that's what's important. I was concerned about what the character looked like, but I worked hardest on the story."

At the Walter Lantz studios, Jack Hannah, who had left Disney after directing many of the Donald Duck cartoons, created Fatso Bear, a character a little like Humphrey the Bear, and which became the preliminary version of Hanna-Barbera's Yogi Bear. The unnamed Disney ranger was transformed into Ranger Willoughby, named for the street that was one of the borders of the Lantz studios. But, Hannah and Lantz weren't yet through with the street. In 1960, they created Inspector Willoughby who sleuthed his way on secret missions in a dozen productions during a six-year career.

A nursery rhyme sparked the names for Lantz's contribution to the cat-and-mice game. The mice were named Hickory and Dickory; the cat was Doc, clothed somewhat like a medicine show doc. All of them were directed by Hannah and Alex Lovy in seven cartoons between 1959 and 1962.

A novelty tune had led to the name of Elmer Fudd; a novelty tune led to the naming of two dogs, Jeepers and Creepers, directed by Seymour Kneitel at Famous Studios. The dogs lasted for only four cartoons in 1960 before being transformed into the humans Swifty and Shorty who reached their popularity in 1964.

A housing subdivision in the New Rochelle-Scarsdale, New York, area, itself named after an English town, became the basis for the name of Hector Heathcote, a Revolutionary War character who starred in thirty-five cartoons from Terrytoons between 1959 and 1963, then appeared in endless re-runs on Saturday morning on television. Bill Weiss, president of Terrytoons when Hector was created, says that the character developed from an Eli Bauer story, *The Minute and a Half Man*—"We used the name Heathcote, but I don't remember why we decided upon it. The first name was something that would be alliterative with Heathcote."

The names of a politician and two Biblical figures were appropriated for characters created by Gene Deitch in the 1950s. The full name for Clint Clobber was DeWitt Clinton Clobber, the "superintendent and sanitary engineer of the Flamboyant Arms Apts." Deitch says that the "full glory of the DeWitt Clint on reference to the popular New York politician of the early nineteenth century made an amusingly pompous contrast to the slob of a super Clobber really was." Many individuals in the Industry believe that the characterization of Clobber, who did what his name said he was supposed to do, came from Jackie Gleason's Ralph Kramden characterization. Deitch, however, says that the characterization was "an attempt to humanize a role that our cameraman Doug Moye used to voice as Papa Bear of the Terrybears. Doug had a booming, raspy voice which sounded quite funny."

The Biblical characters Deitch appropriated were Samson and Delilah who became Samson Scrap and Delilah, stars of three cartoons. Samson Scrap was a junk dealer; Delilah was his horse who pulled the junk wagon. "In that title and those names," says Deitch, "I had alliteration, information as to the trade of the character, and a reference to something known, which implied a love relationship [between a man and his horse]."

Movies and movie actors and actresses often inspired cartoon stories and cartoon names.

The Fleischer Studio seldom based its names upon other names. But, the Fleischers had a contract with Paramount, and Paramount was calling many of the directions. One of those directions was that the Fleischers would call their second feature-length cartoon, *Mr. Bug Goes to Town*. The reasoning was that since Paramount had a successful live-action feature, *Mr. Deeds Goes to Town*, the similarity of the title would help the animated feature. The Fleischere objected; Paramount prevailed; the feature flopped.[6] (Other animated skunks were Snuffy, created in 1932 at the Walter Lantz Studios; Flower, Walt Disney's lovable skunk in *Bambi*; and Li'l Tinker, created in the late 1940s by Tex Avery at MGM.)

A name for a Groucho Marx film provided the inspiration for Quentin Quail, a Warner Brothers character who starred in *The Crackpot Quail* (1941), directed by Tex Avery, with story by Rich Hogan; and *Quentin Quail* (1946), directed by Chuck Jones, with story by Tedd Pierce. The Groucho Marx character was named S. Quentin Quale who appeared in *Go West* (1940). Irv Brecher originated the name, combining the name for a California maximum security prison; slang for a girl, Quail; and the combined slang name for underage girls who, because of legal problems that could result, were often known as San Quentin Quail.

Pepe LePew, the odiferous amorous skunk with a phony romantic French dialect, made his debut in *The Odor-able Kitty* (1945). Pepe was named and developed by Chuck Jones and Mike Maltese from the Charles Boyer characterization of Pepe le Moko in *Algiers*, a remake of the 1937 French film, *Pepe Le Moko*.

In *Swooner Crooner*, a 1945 Warner Brothers cartoon directed by Frank Tashlin, a brilliant animation director who would later become one of the Industry's best live-action directors, bobby-soxer hens leave their nest to swoon over a Sinatra-like rooster, thus causing a work stoppage at the Flockheed Aircraft.

Foghorn Leghorn, the loud-speaking pompous braggart of a rooster who became a star under Bob McKimson's direction, owes his name, his characteristics, and his very existence to two radio shows. On the *Blue Monday Jamboree Radio Show*, a character known as the Sheriff was slightly deaf and believed that other people couldn't hear him talk, so he would repeat himself—"Hello? I said *Hello*, son!" That became one small part of the characterization—the rest was embedded in the characterization of Sen. Claghorn, the fictionalized loud-mouthed pompous braggart of a politician on segments of Fred Allen's popular radio show, known as "Allen's Alley." Both characters were created by Kenny Delmar. Foghorn starred (usually with Charlie Dog, Henry Hawk or Prissy) in from one to three cartoons a year between 1946 and 1962, beginning with *Walky Talky Hawky*.

Walter Lantz went to the movies to create Maw and Paw, two hillbillies who bore uncanny resemblances to Ma and Pa Kettle, portrayed by Marjorie Main and Percy Kilbride in several popular movies. However, the movies lasted longer than the cartoons; after four cartoons were produced during 1953 and 1954, the series was killed.

Mario Puzo's novel *The Godfather*, which spawned an extremely popular film, also spawned a cartoon series, *The Dogfather* (1974-1976). However, the DePatie-Freleng series—even with Freleng, Bob McKimson, Hawley Pratt, Gerry Chiniquy, Sid Marcus, Art Leonardi, and Dave DeTiege directing—was unable to sustain a continuing interest in a family of crime dogs, and was cancelled after only seventeen episodes.

When Peter Benchley's *Jaws* became a monster hit, first as a book then as a movie, it was inevitable that there would soon be imitation jaws. Thus, it was no surprise when myriad books about sharks, or other "violent" animals appeared on the market; and it was no surprise when films followed, and childrens' games and even cartoons. DePatie-Freleng and Hanna-Barbera both brought out imitation jaws during the 1976-1977 television season. DePatie-Freleng's jaws was *Mister Jaw: Supershark*, a land-based shark who wore a top hat and bowtie. At Hanna-Barbera, jaws was Jabberjaw, created by Joe Ruby and Ken Sears, two of the better animator-writers in the Industry. To give the character a continuing role that would appeal to the Saturday morning TV set, Ruby and Sears made Jabberjaw a companion to four teenage musicians who live underwater in the early twenty-first century. However, while *Jaws*—the original *Jaws*—was still playing in theaters, scaring people, and making the author quite happy—first Mister Jaw (1977) then Jabberjaw (1978) received terminal contracts.

Bob Clampett, during more than four decades in the Industry, gleefully "modified" numerous names. In 1946, at Warners, he ingeniously intertwined the title of a famous book with the name of a superstar. The result was *Bacall to Arms*, the story of a wolf who visits a theater and becomes inflamed with screen actress Laurie B. Cool, an animated version of Lauren Bacall. (Clampett sketched from the feature *To Have and to Have Not*, starring Bacall and Humphrey Bogart, now known as Humphrey Go-Cart.)

But most of the best Clampett pun-names were those which kept audiences laughing at his television shows throughout the 1950s, 60s and 70s. Among the characters were Dishonest John (Nya Ha Ha!), lion Mouth Full O'Teeth Keith, Ping Pong (the Giant Ape), Eartha Kitty, the Little Goose (who lost his "muddow"), Sir Cuttle-Bones Jones, the Inca Dinka Doo Bird (patterned after Jimmy "Schnozola" Durante), Mama Llama, Flush Gordon and dog Groucho Barks.

And for the *Beany & Cecil* network cartoon series there were new character and name creations, including Lil Ace from Outer Space, Swordfish Jack the Knife, Davey Crickett and his Leading Lady-Bug, Ol' Spot the Spotted Leopard, Peter Cotton Pickin' Tail, Ben Hare, Snorkel shaped Snorky, Normal

*Bob Clampett's*

# THUNDERBOLT

*(The Wonder Colt)*

*Blunderhead* is the world's smallest horse, no larger than a chipmunk. But one day he met a genie, who gave him a "super suit" with magical powers. And in his "super suit," little Blunderhead becomes *Thunderbolt The Wonder Colt* — Defender of The Animal Kingdom — possessed with super strength, super vision, and the courage of a lion. Like a bolt of lightning, he flashes through the sky to rescue those in trouble, to protect the unprotected.

© Bob Clampett

Norman, lil Homer (one of the "20,000 Little Leaguers Under the Sea") and underwater stars Yogi Barracuda, Ty Codd, Mickey Manta, Joe DeMackeral, Leo DeRoker, Minnow Minosa and Casey Stingeray. From the ranks of the "famous" came Albert Rabbitstein (discoverer of the theory of rabbitivity) and "brain not brawn" advocates Hare-istotle and Hare-cules (who sits under a spreading Chemistree to do some nuclear fission), and canine movie stars Clara Bowlegs, Marilyn Mongrel, Bridget BowWow, Francis X. Bushytail, Boney Curtis, Arlene Dalmation, Eva Marie St. Bernard and Rin-Tin-Can.

Also introduced to audiences were Indian scout Pop Gunn, Baby Ruthy, Bob Newheartburn, Daniel Boon-doggle, Gnat King Cole, Pat O'Bruin (a member of the Unbearables), Pat Swoon, Sir Basil Metabolism, Shirley Dimple, Peking Tom Cat, the singing Dina Sor, an ape named Sam Simeon, The Indiscreet Squeet and the Phantom of the Horse Opera.

For his parody of Walt Disney's *Snow White and the Seven Dwarfs* Clampett created and named *So What and the Seven Whatnots* (with Cecil as Prince Chow-mein), and dwarfs Elf-is, Fred McFurry, Lover-ace, Harpo-like Harpsy McChord, Dizzy R. Nez, Screwloose Latrec and "Stash-Dough" (Louis Armstrong).

Even fellow animators Walt Disney and Walter Lantz weren't safe from Clampett who created Mickey Moose, Stinker Bell (a skunk of an agent), and Woodly Woodwrecker.

Horse names also fascinated Clampett. After completing his Charlie Horse cartoon, which also featured faithful filly Hay-dy La Mare and movie director Gregory Retake, Clampett created the puppet Blunderhead, son of Flicker out of Snicker, names he developed by combining the names of two well-known movie horses, Thunderhead and Flicka. Blunderhead, who could change into Thunderbolt the Wondercolt and fly to the rescue often faced William Shakesepare Wolf, a stage-struck villain.

The fertile and zany mind of satirist Jay Ward conceived two unlikely pairs of animals. In the late 1940s, Ward introduced the dubious combination of a rabbit and a tiger. Raglan T. Tiger (popularly known as Rags the Tiger), Crusader

Bullwinkle J. Moose
Rocket J. (Rocky) Squirrel

Rabbit's happy-go-lucky sidekick in one of television's first continuing animated programs, was named by Ward for a sleeve and a song. The sleeve was Raglan, itself named for Baron Raglan, a nineteenth century nobleman; the song was the popular *Tiger Rag.*

Slightly more than a decade later, Ward—with Pete Burness, Bill Hurtz, Lew Keller, Ted Parmlee and Bill Scott now working with him—combined a plucky flying squirrel and a not-so-bright moose and named them Rocket J. (Rocky) Squirrel and Bullwinkle J. Moose. Bullwinkle took his name from Clarence Bulwinkle (with a single "l"), a used car dealer in Berkeley, California.

"Jay thought Bulwinkle's name was hilarious," recalls Helen Hanson, former production manager for the Jay Ward Studios. Rocky was chosen as "just a square-sounding kid's name... 'Rocky' was then being popularized by prizefighter Rocky Graziano. Besides, Rocky's full name was a tribute to his blinding speed." It is no coincidence that both characters share the middle initial "J." By the time the series was aired, Jay Ward had placed much of himself into it.

Jay Ward and Bill Scott also put themselves into the personalities of Gidney and Cloyd, the two disappearing moonmen who competed with, and also helped, Rocky and Bullwinkle find the elusive "Mooseberry Bush." According to Scott, "Jay and I decided that the two names we would least like to have were Floyd and Sidney. For the moonmen, we just changed the first letters."

But Ward and Scott weren't the only ones to become animated. Bill Hurtz, who has directed the Jay Ward cartoons since 1959, says, "We had a habit of naming our characters for people around us." Thus it shouldn't be considered unusual for the names of a distributor and an apartment building to be transformed not only in the character of a bumbling but lovable Navy captain who could never get his directions straight, but also into the name of his ship. The captain was Capt. Peter (Wrong-Way) Peachfuzz; the origin was Peter Piech who directed the company which distributed Jay Ward's cartoons. The apartment building where Jay Ward maintained a residence and an office was the Andalusia Arms; Capt. Peachfuzz's ship became the S.S. Andalusia.

The names of Chauncy and Edgar, two long-time "townsfolk" who often discussed what was happening to Bullwinkle's Frostbite Falls, were developed, according to Bill Scott, "because we wanted a couple of names for incidental characters who would each have only one name. Those two were ones that I thought people would remember even if they didn't appear except occasionally."

Boris Badenov, Rocky and Bullwinkle's nemesis and "all-around nogoodnik," owed his name to Modest Mussorgsky's opera *Boris Godunov*. The cartoon name was a natural. It had political and phonological significance (it sounded foreign) and it had semantic significance ("bad enough"). It was also alliterative. Boris' cohort, Natasha Fatale, was a sexy femme fatale whose name, like that of Boris, was meant to conjure up images of cold war spies.

Boris appeared in a number of disguises with very revealing aliases, although the naive heroes were always fooled. (Rocky: "That voice. Where have I heard that voice before?") Boris appeared as Ace Rickenboris, a crooked airline pilot; Abou ben Boris, a wily desert chieftain; Colonel Tom Parkoff, a Russian manager of rock stars; Baby Face Braunschweiger, a 1930s Chicago-style hood; D.W. Grifter, a Hollywood talent scout; Captain Horatio Hornswaggle, the pirate captain of the "Maybe Dick"; Sir Rulion Blue, an art buyer; Honeychile Moosemoss (Boris with a southern accent); Mojave Max, G.O.P. (for Grizzled Old Prospector); and Hemlock Soames, a detective for the electric company. (Natasha played Dr. Watkins.)

Jay Ward's mild-mannered Henry Cabot Henhouse, III (named for statesman Henry Cabot Lodge) when confronted by crime, turns into superhero Superchicken who is plagued by villains Dr. Chicago, a mad dentist from Illinois; and Salvadore Rag Dali, a demented toy manufacturer.

The girlfriend of Dudley Do-Right, the bumbling Canadian mountie, was named Nell because, says Lloyd Turner, one of the show's writers, "all melodrama heroines were called Nell, it seemed."

The Ward-Scott team also developed *George of the Jungle*, a superspoof of all the adventure shows then proliferating the screen. According to Bill Scott, "For our characterization of the bumbling apeman, we needed the flattest sounding, non-jungle name in the world. George was it." George's companion was named Ursula, "a longing reminder of Ursula Andress doing some dumb jungle queen role," but George always called her "Fella." Although the characterization may have been that of Ursula Andress, or any of dozens of blonde sultry sex-objects, the name was appropriated from a two-year-old girl. Bill Hurtz, who was responsible for naming the companion, says, "My daughter had a friend named Ursula, and the way [my daughter] said the name it was funny. So, we used it." However, Ursula had originally been called Jane, but, says Hurtz, "We were forced to change it because of the similarity of the Edgar Rice Burroughs characters. So, when my daughter said 'Ursula,' I knew that name was as far away from Jane as you could get."

Although there was objection to the use of the name "Jane" for the Tarzan spoof, apparently no one voiced strong enough objections to prevent Hanna-Barbera from producing *Jana of the Jungle* (1978), the story of a girl who returns to the jungle to search for her father. And, naturally, no one from the Edgar Rice Burroughs estate objected to Filmation studios creating weekly episodes of *Tarzan, Lord of the Jungle* (1976-1978), especially since Filmation had a license from the Burroughs' estate.

And, apparently, no one, including author Ian Fleming, had objections to Terrytoons creating in the mid-1960s dog-spy James Hound. There were also no objections to Filmation producing *The Secret Lives of Waldo Kitty* (1975-1976), loosely based upon James Thurber's delightful story of Walter Mitty, a man who transforms himself into a variety of heroic roles. In the Filmation version, which combined live action with animation, an ordinary common housecat was, in fact, an ordinary common cat. However, when the cat began to fantasize, especially when in trouble, it turned to a world of fantasy and entered the realm of animation.

Mike Maltese, who became a part of Hanna-Barbera long after Warner Brothers issued its last cartoon, brought back some old Loony Tune-like habits and created a pair of characters which he gleefully named Quick Draw McGraw, a

©Jay Ward

Ursula, George, Shep

Babba Looey and Quick Draw McGraw

Western sheriff-hero patterned somewhat upon Red Skelton's characterization of Sheriff Deadeye; and Baba Looey, a quick-thinking companion to the sometimes-dimwitted Quick Draw. "Baba Looey," says Maltese, "was named after the song identified with Desi Arnaz, *Baba Loo*." In several episodes, Quick Draw McGraw, while retaining most of the Sheriff Deadeye personality, took on a superhero role, becoming known as El Kabong, a feared crusader of justice who, with his cape and guitar, which he wasn't afraid to use to "kabong" evil-doers, bore a somewhat unremarkable resemblance to Walt Disney's Zorro.

Another crime fighter with a cape was Dracula, Jr., son of Count Dracula, known as "Big D" in Hanna-Barbera's *Drak Pack* shows which premiered in the 1980-1981 television season. In addition to Dracula, Jr., the Drak Pack (occasionally referred to as a Dreg Pack by Dr. Dred, the evil arch-villain) included Frankie who could become a super-strength Frankenstein monster; and Howard who could become the wolfman. Dr. Dred's gang were the generically-named Vampira, Fly, Mummy Man and Toad.

Blab, the mouse detective partner of the cat detective Super Snooper, also had a name origin at Warner Brothers. Maltese says that "Hanna-Barbera tried naming him Blabber Mouse, after a Warner's character [of the early 1940s] they weren't using any more, but when I called them, they indicated they still had copyright protection on the character. So, we called our character Super Snooper and Blab and there wasn't any problem."

But when Maltese set about to create the characters and names for television's first half-hour animated series, he and Hanna-Barbera found some unexpected problems. According to Maltese, Joe Barbera had developed a concept of a prehistoric cave-dwelling family—a young couple with a kid and a dog, a concept not too unlike that which led to the production of twelve "Stone Age" cartoons by the Fleischer Studio in 1940, or maybe the Dagwood-Blondie concepts. Maltese says, "I told Joe that these characters were too much like Blondie and Dagwood, and I suggested copying Jackie Gleason's *Honeymooners* and having a middle-aged couple with no kids or dog, but with an Art Carney-like next-door neighbor. Joe agreed, and I came up with the title, *Rally 'Round the Flagstones*. Joe thought it was pretty good, but came back to me a little later and said that the title was too long and we'd have to change it to *The Flagstones*." Quickly, a massive publicity campaign was launched, and production begun on the television series patterned after *The Honeymooners*. However, Mort Walker, the creator of the *Hi and Lois* cartoon panels, saw the publicity and felt that the name *Flagstone* was too close to the last name of his characters, *Flagston*—without the *e*. Ted Hannah of King Features, which syndicated the cartoon panels, says that Walker "asked King Features its opinion and the syndicate concurred, writing to Hanna-Barbera pointing out the similarity of names."

Maltese wanted to keep the original name, but he recalls that Barbera told him, "No, we don't want to have any trouble right now. Let's think of another name'." So, Maltese walked out of his office, and halfway down the hall he thought of two stones rubbing together—two *flint* stones. Barbera approved the name change, and Fred and Wilma Flagstone became Fred and Wilma Flintstone, stars of one of the most popular cartoon series in the history of television. "We could have called them anything," says Maltese—"The Rockfords ... or whatever. This one just happened to work."

Hanna-Barbera was luckier when it appropriated the names and personalities of actors and actresses for many of their characters in the series. The Flintstones, living in prehistoric Bedrock, were often visited by twentieth century celebrities with prehistoric names. Among the visitors who crossed the time barrier were Ann Margrock, Cary Granite, Peter Gunite and Rock Pile.

But the problems weren't over for Hanna-Barbera. Shortly after Hanna-Barbera introduced Yogi Bear, Jellystone's "smarter-than-the-average-bear," baseball player Yogi Berra threatened to sue for, among other things, defamation of character. (Ironically, although the name undoubtedly came from Yogi Berra, the characterization was basically that developed by Art Carney for the production of Ed Norton in *The Honeymooners*.) An executive producer for Hanna-Barbera swears that, "We never even thought of Yogi Berra when we named Yogi Bear. It was just a coincidence."

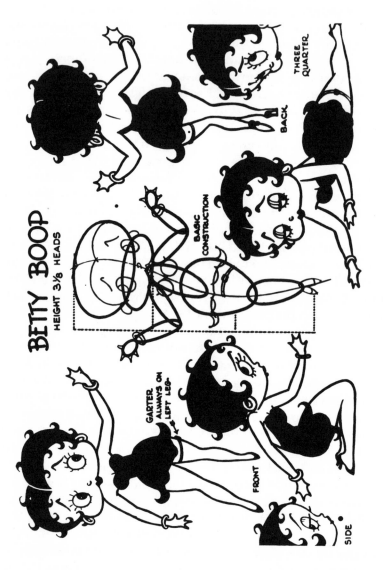

Betty Boop model sheet, 1933

Whether coincidence or not, it is difficult to find anyone else in the Industry who believes it. As one top producer said, "If there was no Yogi Berra, I seriously doubt that there would have been a Yogi Bear. It's just too much of coincidence for me." Nevertheless, Berra's suit never went to court.

In a similar Hanna-Barbera "coincidence," two of the characters of *Where's Huddles?*, a short-lived thirty-minute television series, were named "Bubba" and "Freight Train." Two outstanding football players—Charles (Bubba) Smith and Dick (Night Train) Lane—were well-known when *Where's Huddles?* premiered in the Summer of 1970.

## Lawsuits

Although Yogi Berra once threatened suit, and other athletes who found themselves partially immortalized on celluloid may have given serious thought to lawsuits; Helen Kane was angry enough to take her fight to court. In the 1920s, she was a well-known vaudeville star whose "Boop-oop-a-Doop" and accompanying gestures were almost universally known. In 1931 Grim Natwick, a storyman for the Fleischer Studio, created Betty Boop, whose stature and qualities in animation soon matched, then exceeded, those of Helen Kane in vaudeville.

Natwick recalls that "One morning, they put on my desk a copy of the 'Boop-oop-a-Doop' song sung by Helen Kane. Like so many girls of that time, she wore spit curls. So, I started with that and designed a little character who was supposed to work with Bimbo the Dog. She started out as a little dog with long ears, but the rest of her was extremely feminine." Betty Boop eventually evolved into the first truly feminine character in animation, having undergone the metamorphosis from lady-like dog to sexy and alluring woman. The Fleischers even had a prototype that Natwick could have worked with—Betty Coed, a sexy alluring woman, never became a star, but appeared on a model sheet; the sheet and her first name were copyrighted.

Nevertheless, Miss Kane wasn't flattered by a too-similar image and brought a $250,000 suit against Paramount-Publix Corp., the Fleischers' distribution company, charging that the Fleischer studio had stolen both the name and the characterizations. Shamus Culhane, who animated Betty Boop, says that although there "was concern at Paramount, it didn't affect production one bit." Kane eventually lost the suit when it was proved in court that she had taken the basic "Boop-oop-a-doop" characteristics from another vaudeville star, Baby Esther. In a brief decision handed down May 6, 1934, a week after trial began, and two years after the suit was filed, the New York Supreme Court ruled that none of Miss Kane's civil rights had been violated, and that Max Fleischer's Betty Boop cartoons did not present a case of unfair competition, as Miss Kane had charged.[7]

Mighty Mouse, which had brought a new vitality to the Paul Terry studios during the 1940s, as well as a new 20th Century Fox contract, was originally developed as a hybrid of a common house fly and Superman. According to pioneer animator-writer Isidore Klein, "It had crossed my mind that a 'take-off' of the new . . . comic strip sensation 'Superman' could be the subject for a . . . cartoon. Since most of the animated cartoon characters of that period were humanized animals and insects, I decided on a super-fly."

Klein says that the idea of a superfly appealed to him because "I had read that a fly, for its size, had super strength. With cartoon license, this fly's strength could be multiplied many times over. I warmed up by sketching a fly wearing a super-man type of cape holding up with one arm an enormous pole, which related to his size, seemed like a telegraph pole. He was really balancing an ordinary pencil. In a second sketch, this fly in superman cape was flying against the front of an automobile, causing the radiator to buckle and bringing the car to a forced halt."[8]

Paul Terry looked over the sketches, liked what he saw, but decided to change the character into a mouse. Thus was born Super Mouse who first appeared in *The Mouse of Tomorrow*, released on October 16, 1942.

According to a well-entrenched legend in the Industry, early in 1943, after three or four cartoons were created, Super Mouse was renamed Mighty Mouse when Jerry Siegel and Joe Schuster, who had created Superman in 1938, and the Fleischer Studio, which had first animated the man of steel in

1941, threatened suit for, among other reasons, name infringement. There is a strong possibility that Siegel, Schuster and the Fleischer Studio did query the Paul Terry studio and express concern about both the name and characterization of Mighty Mouse. However, Bill Weiss, who had been at Terrytoon since 1929 and would become its president in the 1950s, says that the creators and distributors of Superman did not ask that Mighty Mouse be re-named. According to Weiss, the reason the name was changed was "because of a problem [that arose] when one of our employees left us and went to work for a comic book outfit, and took the name, Super Mouse, with him. The comic book was in print before us. They used Super Mouse, so we had to change the name; besides, when you have Superman and Super Mouse, there's really no creativity there."

Bluto, half of one of the most violent combinations in animation history, fought with Popeye in comic strips, then in film during the 1930s and 1940s, only to lose his name in 1960 when King Features Syndicate bought all rights and decided to create additional Popeye cartoons. A persistent belief in the Industry suggests that Bluto's name was changed to Brutus because of its supposed similarity to Mickey Mouse's dog Pluto. However, since Walt Disney didn't complain three decades earlier, it's highly unlikely that the Disney organization would now complain. After all, even the most suspicious could hardly find a similarity between a lovable, but often klutzy dog who barks, and a greedy, muscle-bound hulk who, if network standards had permitted, would have sworn blue streaks six minutes straight. Al Brodax, head of the motion picture and film division for the syndicate during the production of the "new" Popeye cartoons, has another explanation. According to Brodax, the syndicate's legal counsel suggested that Bluto's name, apparently the only name in the series under copyright to the Fleischers, who had first animated the Popeye characters and who created the character Bluto, be changed to prevent possible legal problems. It's possible that in legal discussions, the name similarity to Pluto did come up, and may have been considered by the counsel, but it was not a significant reason for the change. Brodax says that the name

Brutus was based upon the name of Julius Caesar's principal assassin. It's also probable that *Brutus* gave immediate connotations of *brutal*, a characteristic well-entrenched in the personality.

In 1971, Jay Ward and Bill Scott playfully tweaked television announcer Durwood Kirby's nose in a running gag in their highly-popular *Rocky and Bullwinkle* series. The *an* Kirwood Derby was a hat that could make the dumbest animal—our hero, Bullwinkle—become the brightest in the world. Kirby threatened suit, claiming that the creation of the Kirwood Derby was a deliberate invasion of a person's right to commercially exploit his own name—charges not too unlike those filed by Helen Kane four decades earlier. Jay Ward, having enjoyed the pun, agreed to discontinue the gag after the current work in production was completed.

But, with megacorporations taking over the animation industry, the executive suites located far from the creative workrooms, there is a very dominant "feel" for avoiding any kind of problems, for "playing safe." According to Bob McKimson, who had seen the Industry change from one of creativity and excitement to one dominated by business interests, "Everyone is now worried about some kind of a suit, so we try to keep names out of cartoons. It's not like it used to be."

No, indeed, it's not like it used to be.

Rikki Confronts the Cobra in *Rikki-Tikki-Tavi*

Scene from *Mowgli's Brothers*

© 1936 Terrytoons

Farmer Al Falfa and Kiko the Kangaroo
(A scene from *Farmer Al Falfa's Prize Package,* 1936)

Col. Heeza Liar

(A scene from *Heeza Liar in Africa, 1913*)

# 7/ The Outrageous Pun

It has been suggested that writers of outrageous puns should be drawn and quoted. Whatever their fate, the work of these witty punsters often finds its way into cartoon naming.

The first pun-name is now seven decades old. About 1913, John Randolph Bray, one of the most respected of the early pioneers, created for Pathe films the notorious prevaricator Colonel Heeza Liar who starred in twenty-seven cartoons between 1915 and 1917, then again between 1922 and 1925. Many film historians, as well as some pioneer animators, claim that the Colonel was based on Teddy Roosevelt, himself a colonel before becoming a president, a man who boasted of his exploits; but Roosevelt, unlike Bray's colonel, actually did what he said he had done. Others claim that Bray's colonel was based upon Baron Munchausen, a well-known teller of tall tales. Perhaps there was a little of both in Heeza Liar. (The characterization was revived in the mid-1960s when Hooper Productions and Jay Ward studios teamed up to create Commander McBragg, a retired Naval officer.)

Shortly after Col. Heeza Liar made his debut, J.R. Bray created another pun-named character, Otto Luck, who, had he lived in the 1980s would have been called a romantic "air head." The four-episode series began and ended in 1915.

More than a decade before Mickey Mouse was created, Paul Terry, working for J.R. Bray, created Farmer Al Falfa. Not only was the name of the leading character a pun, so was the title of his first cartoon—*Farmer Alfalfa's Cat-Astrophe* (1916). When CBS-TV bought the cartoons in the 1950s, Farmer Al Falfa became Farmer Gray. In 1920 Bray introduced a cat in *The Debut of Thomas Cat*, the first color cartoon. The name, although not the characterization, was used by other animators during the next three decades, and was the first name for the Warner Brothers character who became known as Sylvester.

*113*

Popeye, the spinach-eating sailor from the Elzie Crisler Segar newspaper comic strip, distributed by King Features, made his animation debut in *Popeye the Sailor,* a 1933 Betty Boop cartoon, directed by Dave Fleischer and animated by Seymour Kneitel. Eventually making their appearances with Popeye would be the Oyl family—Olive Oyl, Popeye's sweetheart; Olive's brother, Castor Oyl; and her father, Cole Oyl, all of whom appeared in the comic strip. Popeye's nephews were named Peepeye, Pipeye, Pupeye, and Poopeye, all of whom looked like their uncle, but were treated as Olive Oyl's children.[1] As with Donald Duck's nephews, and Daisy Duck's nieces, perhaps it's best not to ask too many questions.

The only significant pun-name that appeared in the Fleischer's first animated feature, *Gulliver's Travels* (1939), was Count Yerchickens. However, several pun-names appeared in the second feature-length cartoon, *Mr. Bug Goes to Town,* released in December 1941. The hero, a grasshopper, had a descriptive pun-name, Hoppity; his girlfriend, a bee, was Honey Bee; her father was Mr. Bumble. Thus, Honey's full name was Honey Bee Bumble. Villains were Swat, the fly; Smack, the mosquito; and C. Bagley Beetle.

The Fleischers seldom used puns in their cartoon titles, but the ones they did use were often adept enough to cause just the slightest shudder in the audience. Among the better pun-titles for the *Out of the Inkwell* series, featuring Koko the Clown, were *Koko-Nuts* and *Koko Gets Egg-Cited.* For one of the cartoons in the *Talkartoons* series, the Fleischers used *Chess-Nuts.* The only pun-title in the *Betty Boop* series was *So Does an Atomobile,* released in 1939. Many of the titles in the *Popeye* series of 105 cartoons were, in classic Popeye-style, malapropisms. Among the better puns were *Strong to the Finich, Axe Me Another, My Artistical Temperature, Learn Polikeness* (in which Bluto becomes Prof. Bluteau, a debonoir teacher of manners), *Onion Pacific, Many Tanks* and *Baby Wants a Bottleship.* Perhaps the best of the Fleischer puns titled a "Stone Age" cartoon, featuring a cave age salesman, *The Fulla Bluff Man,* released in 1940.

Most of the names assigned to characters in Walt Disney's *Fantasia* were named only on storyboards or, later, in children's books based upon the film. Of those named, many had pun-names. In "The Dance of the Flowers" segment, the ostrich was named Mlle. Upanova and the alligator was known as Ben Ali Gator; the hippopotamus was Hyacinth Hippo, a descriptive/generic name. The gods of the "Pastoral" segment—Zeus, Bacchus, Vulcan, Apollo, Iris, Morpheus and Diana—retained their classical names. However, Bacchus's donkey was named Jacchus; and the Centaurs had female friends, the Centaurettes. The smallest mushroom, creatively animated by Art Babbitt, was named Hop Low and there were also the Chinese Mandarins and the Blossom dancers. For the "Sorcerer's Apprentice" segment, Mickey Mouse (occasionally called Michael or Michael Mouse by the creative staff—after all, a star must have a formal name) was cast as the sorcerer in what was to be Mickey's grand comeback. The storyboard name of the sorcerer—Yen Sid, *Disney* spelled backward—was an insider's acknowledgment of the close relationship between Mickey and Walt.

Jiminy Crickett, somewhat based upon Cliff Edward's portrayal of Ukelele Ike, was created by Walt Disney as a visual conscience for Pinocchio. Carlo Collodi's story of the wooden marionette who comes to life, was first published in 1881 in several issues of *Il Journale di Bambini [A Children's Journal]* published in Italy, but did not include a visual conscience. According to animator Ward Kimball, "We needed something small and soon came up with a cricket. Then, if you have a cricket, it was a split second before someone said, '*Jiminy* Cricket!' It was a common exclamation at that time." So common, in fact, that in 1937, three years before *Pinocchio,* the seven dwarfs of *Snow White* exclaimed "Jiminy crickets!" when they came home from work to find the lights on in their cottage. (The cat, Figaro, and the goldfish, Cleo, later starred in three separate cartoons in 1943, 1946 and 1947).

Another of the Disney puns was Spike, the bee, who debuted in the 1948 cartoon *Interior Decorator.*

An expression well-known to just about anyone who ever wore military dog-tags was "Situation Normal: All Fucked Up," occasionally bowdlerized to "...fouled up." Nevertheless, most people know it as *Snafu,* a word that came into popular use prior to World War II, but was used continuously since then. When the Army decided to get short messages about such things as malaria protection of problems with leaking secrets across to its soldiers, it created Private Snafu and gave Warner Brothers a contract that led to twenty-two Private Snafu cartoons between 1942 and 1945, all of them

written humorously by Theodore Geisel and directed by the leading Warner Brothers animation directors. When the war ended, Private Snafu was discharged from Warner Brothers.

Tweety, the little yellow canary who was the object of Sylvester's culinary advances, was the brain-child of Bob Clampett.

Just before the war, Bob Clampett and Tex Avery directed *The Cagey Canary*, produced in 1941. The cartoon introduced a canary, its grandma-type mistress, and a black cat.

In 1942, a baby bird appeared in Clampett's excellently-produced *A Tale of Two Kitties*, written by Mike Sasanoff, and featuring two cats named Babbit and Cats-tello, a take-off on the popular actor-comedians, Bud Abbott and Lou Costello. Clampett recalls, "I introduced my little bird in a nest as a foil for the cats, but he stole the show when he said, 'I tot I taw a putty-tat! I did! I did! I taw a putty-tat!'" (The phrase was a slight modification of a much more risque phrase Clampett had created a few years earlier.) Clampett recounts how when he was planning to leave Warner Brothers, in the mid-1930s to film Edgar Rice Burroughs' Mars stories in animation for MGM, he wrote a letter to a musician friend on a sheet of MGM letterhead paper, which bore the familiar Leo the Lion logo. Beside it, he doodled in a baby bird pointing at the lion, saying, "I think I taw a titty-tat!" Clampett's friend wrote back that the members of the band "got quite a kick" out of the "titty tat" gag. "Titty-tat" became "Putty-tat for screen use." (Tweety's innocent stare at the camera and basic design is based in part on Clampett's own nude baby picture.)

After the success of this first Tweety short, Clampett asked for and was granted sole rights to make the Tweety series. It was in the second cartoon, *Birdy and the Beast* (1944), with a story by Warren Foster and animation by Tom McKimson, that Clampett first introduced the name of "Tweety" to the audience. By his fourth year on the screen, Tweety was a well-established cartoon star.

And then a strange thing happened. The censors suddenly exclaimed "Why that bird looks naked!" Rather than put a little pair of Mickey Mouse-like pants on him, Clampett decided to cover Tweety with yellow feathers, and a slimmer body, making him into a canary. Recalling the story line of *The*

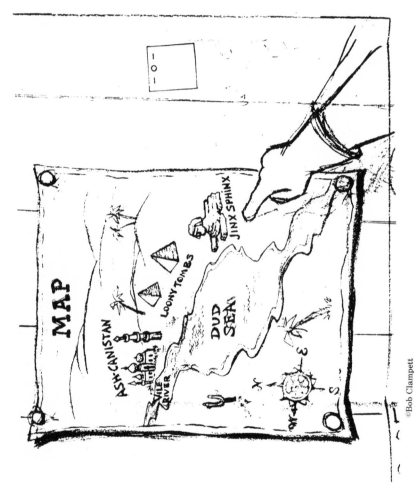

©Bob Clampett

'Let's Check the Map, Beany Boy'

*Cagey Canary,* Clampett decided to do a new version of this general plotline. Having used Sylvester in his 1946 cartoon, *Kitty Kornered,* starring Porky, Clampett decided to team Sylvester with Tweety for the first time in this story which he titled *Tweetie Pie* (a name suggested by Mike Sasanoff and Carl Stalling). When Clampett left Warners to start his own studio, he left behind a number of projects, including some Tweety and Sylvester adventures. Friz Freleng took over the direction of the Tweetie and Sylvester cartoons. *Tweetie Pie* won the Academy Award, the first ever given to a Warner Brothers cartoon. The audience would now be able to choose between MGM's cat-and-mouse chaos, featuring superstars Tom and Jerry, Harvey's Herman and Catnip or Warners' cat-and-canary chases.

In 1947, now with his own studio, Clampett brought Charlie Horse to the screen in *It's a Grand Old Nag,* a character name he had first written about over 15 years earliers; and from the late 1940s throughout the 1950s and into the 60s he was really rolling with Beany and Cecil naming. For his Beany and Cecil cartoon series, Clampett created Tearalong, the Dotted Lion; a beatnik painter Go Man Van Gogh, extra-terrestrial Beepin' Tom; the Guided Muscle Missile; robots from outer space Venus the Meanest and son Venice the Menace (a take-off on Hank Ketcham's "Dennis the Menace"); Billy the Squid; and ducks Graham and Sody Quacker[2] among many, many others.

Some of Clampett's most memorable puns were the places that Cap'n Huffenpuff and his crew of Beany and Cecil often found themselves—the Amos 'n' Andes Mountains, Bedside Manor, Boris' Car Lot, Darn Old Duck Pond, Fun-T-See-Land, Good Grief Reef, Horrors Heights, Hotel Fountain Boo, Jollywood, No Bikini Atoll, Slipping Beauty Castle, Squid Row, the Straits of Jacket, Veronica Lake, and Widow's Peak, among others.

During the 1950s, the Paul Terry studios created several briefly popular but little remembered characters with pun-names—Little Roquefort, a mouse; Gaston Le Crayon, a French artist; and John Doormat, the personification of the meek John Q. Public. The Paul Terry studios in the mid-1950s

FLEBUS

© terrytoons 1957
FOR 20TH CENTURY FOX FILMS

also produced the villain Crabby Appleton—identified to the audience as "rotten to the core"—for the Tom Terrific series on CBS-TV's *Captain Kangaroo* show.

Gene Deitch, who had helped give Terrytoons a creative thrust during the 1950s, liked a character Ernie Pintoff developed, but didn't like the name. "Willie was not memorable enough," says Deitch, who renamed the character the more unusual—and memorable—Flebus, who premiered in 1957. Deitch explains that he developed the name from a disease— "Driving to work one morning, I heard a medical talk show about phlebitis, and it just sounded funny to me. I'm sure it wouldn't have sounded funny if I had the phlebitis! Flebus is just a funny-sounding word-name not having any real meaning at all, but somehow epitomizing the character."

One hundred episodes of Q.T. Hush were produced by Animation Associates for television syndication in 1960 before the appropriately-named sleuth went undercover, appearing only in reruns for the next few seasons.

But at the Jay Ward studios, crime ran rampant for more than a decade as Jay Ward reworked "deadly" into a pair of Dudleys—the villainous Dudley Nightshade, a pun on the poisonous plant; and Dudley Do-Right of the Mounties, the all-time nebbish of a hero. Both names referred to characteristics; in Do-Right's case, it also referred to his personality—a dud.

The essence of Dudley Do-Right was later transformed into some of the essence of race driver Tom Slick. The name was a pun adaptation of Tom Swift and the racing word *slick*, a treadless racing tire. But Tom Slick wasn't his only name. According to Lloyd Turner, "I originally named the character Stretch Marks, and we all laughed and loved it." Eventually, however, the name was shelved for the more racing-sounding Tom Slick.

In 1965, Paramount created Silent Knight, who starred with Honey Halfwitch, in *Baggin' the Dragon*, eleven cartoons in three years.

A few years later, DePatie-Freleng created a thirty-minute television series, *The Barkleys,* the story of a family of English dogs, and loosely based upon the live-action television show *All in the Family.* "Why *not* call a family of English dogs the Barkleys?" asks David H. DePatie.

Popeye

Go Man Van Gogh

Hanna-Barbera also pleaded guilty to the use of outrageous puns. One of their best was Friar Pork, a Friar Tuck-like pig in the feature *Robin Hoodnik*. Whether the name preceded the character, came at the same time or was tacked on after the character was established, is not known.

Equally "outrageous" were the names of leading characters in *The Hillbilly Bears*, a *Beverly Hillbillies* look-alike in animal animation. There were Maw and Paw Rugg and their children, Floral Rugg and Shag Rugg.

Live-action television also inspired another of the many Hanna-Barbera dogs. The character J.J. (portrayed by Comedian Jimmy Walker) on *Good Times* often punctuated extreme happiness with a resounding "Dy-no-MITE!" It was a simple transformation to create bionic dog Dynomutt in 1976. However, the characterization was that of Art Carney's portrayal of Ed Norton.

Hanna-Barbera also created the loquacious duck Yakky Doodle; Mr. Finkerton, the fink of a president of a private investigation service in *Inch High, Private Eye*; and Capt. Skyhook, the nemesis of the space-age *Space Kidettes* gang. But, perhaps, the most outrageous, and certainly one of the wittiest name-puns, was Mike Maltese's Donkey Oatie. "It just came," said Maltese matter-of-factly.

While puns infiltrated character naming, they virtually dominated the titles. According to director Bob McKimson, "We were always looking for puns in our titles. If we wanted a title for something, we'd throw a few titles around, and then somebody [in the studio] might come up with something that was much better, and no matter who it was [who suggested the title], we'd use it."

Chuck Jones, whose cherubic face glows when he talks about puns, created several pun-names for his cats, among them Claude Cat, who first appeared in *The Mouse Wreckers* (1949); Harry Cat in the Chester J. Cricket television series; and Henry Dieux-Claw in *Barnaby Scratch*. But he was at his best creating titles for his cartoons.

The titles Jones, Mike Maltese, and Tedd Pierce gave the Pepe LePew cartoons were often based upon the odorous qualities of the star—*Scent-imental Over You, For Scenti-*

*mental Reasons* (Academy Award, 1949), *Scent-imental Romeo, Two Scent's Worth*, and *The Odor-able Kitty*, among others.

Jones and Maltese are also responsible for *What's Opera, Doc?* (with Bugs murdering opera; the star was Giovanni Jones), *The Rabbit of Seville* (with Bugs and Elmer Fudd murdering opera; Carlo Jonsi was given a credit in the opera-within-a-cartoon, *Hare Tonic* (with Elmer Fudd), *Forward March Hare, Wackiki Rabbit* (Bugs in Hawaii), *Bully For Bugs* (Bugs and a bull), *Rabbit Hood* (Bugs as a defender of the poor); *Rabbit Fire, Martian Through Georgia* and *Mad as a Mars Hare* (Bugs vs. a Martian, namely Marvin the Martian). Other punny titles include *The Scarlet Pumpernickle* (Daffy Duck as a hero), *Water, Water Every Hare, Fast and Fury-ous* (with the coyote), *Scrambled Aches, Naughty but Mice, Hush My Mouse, To Itch His Own* (with the Mighty Angelo, the world's strongest flea), *Much Ado About Nuttin'* (a squirrel desperately tries to open a nut), *A Sheep in the Deep, Sheep Ahoy, Double or Mutton, Claws for Alarm, Louvre Come Back to Me, Cats-bah*, and *Snow Time for Comedy*, among many, many others.

But Friz Freleng was anyone's match when it came to puns. In *Knighty Knight Bugs*, winner of the Academy Award for 1958, Freleng created two bit-player cowardly knights, Sir Loin of Beef and Sir Osis of the Liver.

The titles of DePatie-Freleng's Pink Panther cartoons all included the word "pink." Among the better puns are *Sink Pink, Slink Pink, Pink Aye, Pink Ice, Pinkfinger, Reel Pink, Pink Panzer, Pink-a-Boo, Genie with the Light Pink Fur, Pinknic, Pink of the Litter, The Hand is Pinker than the Eye, Pink Outs, Pinkadilly Circus, Pink-a-Rella, Pink Tuba-Dore* and *Gong with the Pink;* The immortal *Pink Phink*, directed by Friz Freleng, won an Academy Award for the best animated short of 1964.

One of the Industry-wide informal codes, accepted by all, is that one good pun deserves another. Thus, it is not surprising that the better puns often reappear, occasionally modified.

In the early 1950s, Chuck Jones directed *Little Beau Pepe* (1952) and *Bully for Bugs* (1953), both written by Mike Maltese. In 1965, DePatie-Freleng produced *Bully for Pink*, and in 1968, produced *Little Beau Pink*, informal tributes to the genius of

Chuck Jones. And in 1970, Walt Disney produced a full-length feature film, *The Aristocats*. Although the plot and characterization differed, the title was noticeably similar to the 1943 Chuck Jones animated short *The Aristo-cat*.

Nevertheless, throughout the history of animation, just about every animator and writer, from 1913 to the present, has used pun humor to name characters and places, for in an Industry in which the creative mind is often the wild and outrageous mind, and occasionally the repetitive mind, such naming is, after all, only pundamental.

Nell, Horse, Dudley Do-Right

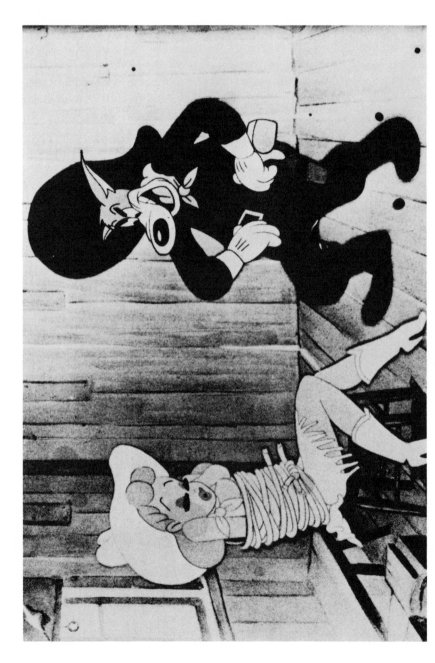

Tex Avery's Wolf
(A scene from *Wild and Wolfy* 1945)

# 8/ The No-Name Names

Like Pluto, Bugs Bunny, Daffy Duck and other cartoon superstars before their rise to stardom, characters in minor roles are seldom named on screen, and even their "working" names, the names used to distinguish them on storyboards, are "throwaways."

In almost every case, when an unnamed cartoon character received even the slightest popularity, it became necessary to give it a name. However, there were exceptions.

None of the characters in Walt Disney's *Skeleton Dance*, which launched the Silly Symphonies series in 1929, were named. And, with only one exception, none of the characters of *Fantasia*, Disney's epic tribute to classical music, were named except on storyboards or later in children's books.[1] But, none needed on-screen names. Wilfred Jackson, one of the directors of the animated features, explains that "the music was paramount. We were told that the music was sacred. We were to do what we could to make the action work without molesting the sound track." The one character who did emerge with a name was Chernobog, the devil. Bill Tytla, whom most in the Industry regard as the leading American animator, was selected to animate the "Bald Mountain" sequence. According to Tytla, "On all my animation, I tried to do research and look into the background of each character. So for the devil . . . I did some reading about Moussorgsky. Now, I'm Ukranian, and Moussorgsy used terms I could understand. He talked about 'Chorni-bok,' the Black Art. Ukranian folklore is based on 'Chorni-bok'—I related to this and studied up."[2] But as Jackson says, "I never did hear that name until the picture was finished. He was just the Devil to us."

As for the name of the picture itself, *Fantasia*, through much of the production, was known as *The Concert Feature*, receiving its permanent name just prior to theatrical release in

1940; Disney had established a contest and offered prizes for the naming of the picture.

Just as Max Hare had perhaps provided the seed of an idea for Bugs Bunny, the Disney wolf of *Three Little Pigs*, released in 1933, provided a skeletal characterization for a Tex Avery wolf which followed him from Schlesinger and Warner's to MGM. Soon it was Avery's wolf that brought the laughs and became one of the film industry's most delightful villains. In 1937, for Schelesinger, Avery directed, from a story by Cal Howard, *Little Red Walking Hood*, starring Egghead as the hero, and featuring an unnamed wolf who steals the show.

The first project Avery did for MGM, in 1942, featured *The Blitz Wolf*, written by Rich Hogan, with animation by Ray Abrams, Preston Blair, Ed Love and Irven Spence, and released in 1943. The cartoon received an Academy Award nomination. The Blitz Wolf, a Hitler-like character, fools two pigs, but not the wise little pig, Sgt. Pork.

In 1943, the wolf becomes a run-away convict—complete with prison stripes—in *Dumb-Hounded,* starring the newly-created Droopy who continually foils the wolf's escape plans. Two months later, the wolf—his personality becoming refined as a Hollywood hipster trickster wolf, always on the make, and always foiled—stars in the sexually-suggestive *Red Hot Riding Hood*, one of the best short cartoons every made.[3] This time the wolf is chasing Red, a torch singer/dancer; he pursues her to Grandma's, where Grandma begins pursuing the reluctant wolf. Later that year, the wolf again pursues pigs in *One Ham's Family*, written by Rich Hogan. The following year, the wolf becomes a pitcher in *Batty Baseball*.

In 1945, the wolf, still unnamed, starred in three cartoons. In *The Shooting of Dan McGoo*, based on a poem by Robert W. Service—the horny wolf chases Lou, a stripper in the Malamute Saloon in Alaska, only to be hounded by the ever-persistent Droopy. In *Swing Shift Cinderella*—written by Allen and animated by Abrams, Blair and Love—the wolf finds himself in a wacky Cinderella parody; and in *Wild and Wolfy*—written by Allen and animated by Abrams, Blair, Walt Clinton and Love—the wolf, Droopy and the girl go "Western."

In 1946, the wolf again becomes a convict and Droopy

becomes a Royal Canadian Mounted Policeman, in *Northwest Hounded Police*. The next year, the wolf returns in the wacky satire *Uncle Tom's Cabana*. This time, the wolf is pursuing torch singer Little Eva, the alluring star of a nightclub (in reality, a cabin) owned by Uncle Tom who is going to fall victim several times to the wolf's devious ways to get rid of the club. Then, two years later, the wolf reappears in the classic *Little Rural Riding Hood*—written by Rich Hogan and Jack Cosgriff, and animated by Bob Cannon, Walter Clinton and Michael Lah—where, as a country wolf, he goes to the city which, as he's been told by his cousin, the city wolf, has an abundance of Riding Hoods. The Riding Hood he focuses on is, of course, a torch singer, the same one who appeared in other wolf pictures.

Later, the wolf would be slightly muted and become the foil for Mighty Mouse in several cartoons where Mighty Mouse rescues a Riding Hood-like girl from danger. And, even later, after Avery had left MGM, William Hanna and Joseph Barbera would direct cartoons in which the wolf becomes a very lovable character with almost no resemblance to the Avery wolf that brought tears of laughter from the audience. It would be this wolf that would eventually evolve into a very unwolflike Huckleberry Hound.

Foxy, directed and produced by Rudy Ising, became the star of the first Merrie Melodies cartoon distributed through Warner Brothers. However, the fox, who bore a resemblance to Mickey Mouse, starred in only three cartoons, all produced in 1931.

For the Van Beuren studio, Shamus Culhane developed another fox, this one a fox terrier who was matched with three unnamed kittens. "We didn't need names for the kittens," says Culhane. "They were all the same." He says that the kittens weren't even identified on the storyboards.

In 1941 Frank Tashlin directed two unnamed characters in *The Fox and the Grapes*, an Aesop fable. The stars, a fox and a crow, slowly developed a following, and between 1941 and 1947 starred in nineteen cartoons produced by UPA, all directed by John Hubley; two received Academy Award nominations.

The Fox and the Crow

The Roadrunner cartoons, which premiered in 1948, were created by Chuck Jones and Mike Maltese, and had the distinction within a decade of being animated classics. Featured in the cartoons were two stars with no names. The elusive roadrunner was simply the Roadrunner, although storyboards identified her as "Mimi." Her antagonist was simply known as the Coyote. It wasn't until 1951 that the coyote was formally named—at least for one episode. The episode was *Operation: Rabbit.* In one scene, the coyote presents Bugs Bunny with a calling card—"Wile E. Coyote, genius." The name was never used on screen again. But the Roadrunner and Coyote cartoons gave birth to a nationwide naming phenomenon. During the 1960s, "Roadrunner" became the nickname for Maury Wills, the fleet-footed base-stealer for the Los Angeles Dodgers; the name for a sporty

Coyote Model Sheet

Roadrunner Model Sheet

The Coyote and the Roadrunner

model in the Plymouth automobile line; and everything from cafes to trucking companies.

Shortly after the Roadrunner cartoons went out of production, in 1968 (after DePatie-Freleng took over production from Warner Brothers four years earlier), DePatie-Freleng created a tamer roadrunner spin-off. Instead of a roadrunners, there was now a giant ant. Instead of a coyote, there was now a blue aardvark, both of which talked, giving a different dimension to their personalities. "We never considered giving names to the ant and aardvark," said David H. DePatie, "because people would just like to remember them in their simple form."

Friz Freleng says, "We would have named them if there was a reason in the stories, but there wasn't any opportunity to give them names."

The Tasmanian Devil, a marsupial indigenous to the island of Tasmania, located southwest of Australia, became the basis of the Tasmanian Devil, the wild whirling nemesis of Bugs Bunny. According to Bob McKimson, who directed the Tasmanian Devil cartoons, "I was working with Sid Marcus, and we were looking for a character for a miscellaneous cartoon. We were kicking around concepts using different animals and birds. And, just kidding, we came up with the idea that the only thing left was the Tasmanian Devil." McKimson explains that he "worked a lot of crossword puzzles and these things [the Tasmanian Devil] came up every once in a while, and it was just at a time when one came up in one of those puzzles. Sometimes, selecting and naming characters is just that simple."

The Tasmanian Devil—now an identified and popular character—later received a personal name. According to McKimson, "Someone wrote in and wanted a picture of the Tasmanian Devil, and in the letter called him Taz Boy. From then on I called him Taz Boy because it was so descriptive of him."

The Cat starred in four cartoons between 1960 and 1961, all of them directed by Seymour Kneitel and produced by Famous Studios. The Cat was a British private detective, patterned on the characterization of Cary Grant, but was never named.

Jay Ward and Bill Scott gave George of the Jungle a

sidekick named Ape. "We named him 'Ape' to remind people that he really was an Ape, because he talked and behaved like Ronald Coleman," says Bill Scott.

Lloyd Turner, one of Jay Ward's top writers, put a non-name into the Dudley Do-Right cartoons. Turner says, "We named Dudley's horse, Horse. That's obvious. That's what he was."

### No-Names and the Ads

Beginning in the early 1950s and continuing through the present, animation has become a vital part of many television commercials. In most instances, animation is only a small part, perhaps to illustrate a new product; in some instances, the commercial spawns talked-about characters, some of whom are named.

Harry and Bert—two all-American characters with all-American names—appeared in thirty commercials for Piel's Beer between 1955 and 1960, then were resurrected in the early 1980s, much to the joy of Piel's distributors. Howard Beckman, who animated Harry and Bert, says that they are two of his favorite characters.

However, the representative of the Olympia Brewing Co., the Hamm's Beer bear, who was forever getting into trouble in his forest homeland, was not named. The bear first appeared in 1954, and was extremely popular for over a decade. When Heublein bought out Hamm's, the bear went into retirement— and sales dropped. Then, in 1978, with Olympia the new owner, the bear made a spectacular comeback. Michael Kilpatrick, of Olympia, says that, "We never seriously discussed naming him. It was part of the mystique."

A bird with no-name was the VIB bird (for Very Important Bird) from Western Airlines. Like the Hamm's bear, VIB bird made its debut in the mid-1950s, became extremely popular for a decade as it rode on top of airplanes in business-executive comfort, and told television audiences that Western was "the *oh-o-nly* way to fly," then was forced into retirement. A brief comeback in the late 1970s brought happiness to Western personnel as well as the television public, but the bird was dropped once again.

Hamm's Beer Bear

VIB Bird

Breakfast cereal companies, which sponsor Saturday morning cartoons, have found that it is logical for their own commercials to feature cartoon characters. For several decades, Kellogg's had Snap, Crackle and Pop, descriptive elf-like characters who promoted Rice Krispies, and were named because the company wanted to make sure that the public, and especially the younger public, knew that their cereal made noises. When Kellogg's entered television, so did the characters. Later the company developed Tony the Tiger whose mission was to let everyone know that there was strength in Sugar Frosted Flakes every time he proclaimed they were "GGRRRRREAT!" For Sugar Crisps, Bill Tytla animated cute, but unnamed, bears. Cap'n Crunch (and the Crunchberry), animated by Jay Ward studios, was named by the advertising agency after extensive marketing research—after all, Cap'n Crunch was the representative of a brand-name cereal bearing his name, and an agency's client can't have just *any* name that comes to mind.

Charlie the Tuna, who was forever devising elaborate ploys to become a Star-Kist tuna, only to be repeatedly told, "Sorry, Charlie," has helped Star-Kist into a top slot as a tuna processor. Although Charlie, animated by DePatie-Freleng, was named—the scripts called for a name—the mermaid who represented Chicken of the Sea was left unnamed, though bearing a remarkable similarity to the mermaid who watches over Copenhagen.

The Frito Bandito, complete with sombrero, six-shooters and straps of bullets slung across his body, appeared for a few years, then was dropped when the Chicano communities began protesting the stereotyped image the Bandito presented.

Apparently no giants protested the image of the Jolly Green Giant, a gentle giant who walked the land to promote processed vegetables. And neither did spiders and other "bugs" protest the evil image presented by the bug spray companies. To illustrate the destructive power of their products, both Raid and Black Flag went to animation after marketing studies suggested that using real bugs as victims wasn't going to be accepted by the usually-squeemish audience. The result was the use of animated cockroaches and other "creepy crawlers" who were efficiently, and neatly, overcome. Raid used Tex Avery on the West Coast to illustrate its product, and Avery, whose sight gags with Warner Brothers and MGM gave him the reputation of being one of the top directors in the Industry, gave Raid what it wanted—an amused, happy audience that bought Raid—and thought that bugs were evil. On the East Coast, Howard Beckerman animated bugs for Black Flag. "At first, they were just cute bugs who were pests," says Beckerman, "but as we produced more and more cartoons, I managed, a little at a time, to add personalities to them. But we never named them. Not even on storyboards."

Educational films usually have identifiable characters, but very few given names. According to Stephen Bosustow, one of the leading educational film animator-producers, "We don't do much naming in these films because there's no need to develop the character."

And that's probably the key to the no-names in animation—if there's no need to develop the character, there's usually no need to develop the name.

Raid Bugs

(Bob Clampett collection)

Title Cards

# 9/ Forbidden Names

A number of Industry-wide codes, written and unwritten, dictate what can and can't appear on screen. The primary categories that will cause a producer trouble are excessive violence, obscene language and sexual themes. Between 1933 and 1954 when the Hays Office was the Industry's chief censor, animation units made extraordinary attempts to "put one over."

Winston Hibler, one of Walt Disney's leading producers, says, "Get any group of creative people together for the purpose of naming characters and of course the group is going to come up with some blue dialogue and proper names that are highly *im*proper with double and triple meanings. But these names never went beyond the chuckle stage and certainly never reached the Hays Office."

Bob Clampett, the master of the pun, deliberately tweaked the noses of the censors by having Cecil, his seasick serpent, bashfully refer to a robin red-breast as a "robin redvest," then shyly add, "I'm too young to say 'chest'." Clampett recalls that Industry-wide censorship codes were used to force him to change the title on a Porky Pig cartoon which he directed at Warner Brothers in 1937. According to Clampett, he originally titled the cartoon *It Happened All Night*, based on Frank Capra's classic motion picture *It Happened One Night*. It so happened that the title was superimposed over a scene of Porky and Gabby in bed. "The censors got to it and thought it to be too risque," says Clampett with a delightful grin on his face, "so I retitled it *Porky's Bad Time Story*. They didn't object to that!" (The cartoon was remade seven years later as *Tick, Tock, Tuckered,* starring Porky and Daffy.)

The Hays Office got on-screen credit of a sort in the 1942 cartoon, *A Tale of Two Kitties*, directed by Clampett, and featuring a yellow bird. In the cartoon two cats were fighting over the bird. One of the cats demanded, "Give me the bird! Give me the bird!" The other cat retorted, "If the Hays Office would only let me, I'd give him the bird, all right!"

During the "Golden Era" of film—the 1930s and 1940s— the word "buzzard" was taboo because of its presumed connotations. The message did not reach all the film-makers, however, and Clampett created Beaky, a Mortimer Snerd-like bird. The baby buzzard co-starred with Bugs Bunny in *Bugs Bunny Gets the Boid*, released in 1942. "Originally, I just called him the Snerd-bird," says Clampett, "but when I starred him in a second film, Leon Schlesinger asked me to think up a name for him, so I came up with Beaky, which I put on the model sheet, and I titled the cartoon, *The Bashful Buzzard*. If I had known that the word 'buzzard' was censorable, I most likely would have tried to do something anyway. As it was, I didn't know that buzzard wasn't an acceptable name. And no one really said anything."

Beaky Buzzard was a sympathetic character. Buzz Buzzard wasn't. Walter Lantz, who created Buzz Buzzard, Woody Woodpecker's antagonist, says that he had no problems with the censorship codes—"simply because we played him as a heavy, and he always came out the loser with Woody." Other producers—whether they played the buzzard sympathetically or as the loser—usually did have problems with the vacillating code guideline interpretations, and their efforts usually didn't reach the screen.

During the "Golden Age of Animation," even with the Hays Office lurking in the background, naming and character development as well as story development were internal matters, something to be determined by those who made the cartoons. If a character was to be successful or not, it was the audience who decided. But, in the age of television and limited animation, there would be others who helped determine what appeared. They had different names, different titles, were often untrained in the creative arts, but they were all "from the network," and they used a veto power to make creative decisions. Joe Simon, production manager for Filmation, says that the production companies "have been trying to present them [the networks] with new shows, but they don't seem to be interested in original shows." Simon also believes, "They not only restrict the language, but also certain actions." And, they also rule on names.

*Wild Wheels*, a Hanna-Barbera cartoon series about three all-American children involved with motorcycle racing, was renamed *The Devlins*, a more wholesome name. The title wasn't the only thing changed for the half-hour series which premiered in 1974, but experienced a short life. "Our title character was 'Dare' Devlin," says a former Hanna-Barbera producer, "but the network [ABC] made us drop the 'Dare' because of what [it] called 'image problems'." The final name was an inoffensive Ernie Devlin.

The naming guidelines at one of the major cartoon studios forbids the use of the name *Bruce*. An executive of that studio during the mid-1970s, probably reflecting network bias, said that the name wasn't used "because of its homosexual connotations." Other producers for other studios, although not using the character name Bruce, had no such problems. "I certainly don't equate the name Bruce with homosexuality," says one producer. And David H. DePatie raises a social consciousness question. "By deliberately avoiding the use of the name Bruce," he asks, "does a studio reinforce the belief in stereotypes?"

DePatie-Freleng's Spruce, created by Friz Freleng, became Spiffy. According to Freleng, "[Someone] from ABC kept saying, 'Spruce? I don't think kids know what sprucing means. Wouldn't Spiffy sound better?' So we said we didn't care what [they named] them—'Name them anything you want. If it pleases you, we'll call them Spiffy and Fleabag'." Could the network's concern with "Spruce" also have been because of its linguistic similarity to Bruce?—"Possibly."

Eventually, studios will have to confront the problem of whether they wish to put homosexual characters—named Bruce, Roger or anything else—into cartoons. And, one day, they'll have to have an even harder look at ethnic representation in animated cartoons.

Fred and Wilma Flintstone (near side)

# 10/WASP Names

Throughout the history of animated cartoons, there has been a tendency to give human characters names and identification that could be characterized as WASPish. There seems to be an unwritten "rule" perceived by some cartoon producers that humans in animated form should be White. And not only should they be White, they also should have Anglo-Saxon Protestant characteristics; their names should reflect those characteristics.

Names of animated humans, coupled with the characters involved, lead inevitably to the conclusion that people in cartoonland, as well as their audiences, are White, Anglo-Saxon and Protestant. Occasionally, non-human characters have WASP names.

Ward Kimball says that at the Disney studios, "Nothing was made of it [creating WASP names]. But it'd be a built-in ingredient. You would go for a foreign name [only] if you were obviously making a foreign-type picture." One of those pictures was *Don Donald* (1937), a cartoon short directed by Ben Sharpsteen. *Don Donald*—Donald Duck in Spanish motif—featured an attractive female duck, Donna Duck. According to Jack Hannah, a leading Disney director, Donna Duck was selected as a name "because it suggested a Spanish name and also was a natural combination to Don." But, in 1940, in the cartoon *Mr. Duck Steps Out*, Donna Duck became Daisy Duck. According to Kimball, "If you knew the Disney point of view, they probably thought Donna sounded too Spanish. Daisy was more apple pie and American." Disney, however, made effective use of Jose Carioca, a Spanish dancing parrot.

In 1942, Dave Fleischer, for Columbia Pictures, created Tito, a Mexican boy, and his burro, Burrito. There were only three episodes produced over a four-year period, but both characters appeared in other cartoons.

A decade after Columbia created its Mexican boy and burro companion, Warner Brothers created Speedy Gonzales, "the fastest mouse in all Mexico." Speedy made his appearance in *Cat-Tails for Two* (1953). According to Bob McKimson, who directed the first cartoon, the name came from a dirty joke—"A friend of mine told me this joke and the name of the character was Speedy Gonzales. We already had the character developed, but no name. So, the next day I told Warren Foster, my storyman, the joke, and we decided that we'd name the Mexican mouse Speedy Gonzales." McKimson emphasizes that although a dirty joke spawned the name, "At no time was the name ever meant to be derogatory. We had no trouble using a Spanish name—as long as it fit the character."

DePatie-Freleng Enterprises, however, had trouble with the people at Network Standards—the censorship people for the television networks. According to Friz Freleng, *The Tijuana Toads*, which was a hit as a cartoon filler in movie theaters, was banned from television. Freleng says, "We couldn't sell the series to TV because of the ethnic name. We figured we could change the [voice] track, but it wouldn't be funny anymore. The people who loved it the most were the Spanish-American people. They all loved it." Eventually, the voices were redubbed—in variations of Network Standard English—and the series was sold to television in 1976 as *The Texas Toads*. Approved for television, however, were the voices for the ant and the aardvark. The ant had a Dean Martin-sounding voice; the aardvark had a Jewish-sounding Jackie Mason voice.

The leading characters of DePatie-Freleng's *The Barkleys* (1972-1973) were Arnie and Annie Barkley and their children, Terri, Chester and Roger. The following season, DePatie-Freleng produced *Bailey's Comets*; the names were "younger," but they were still WASPy—Barnaby, Candy, Bunny, Sarge, Dude, Pudge and Wheelie.

Friz Freleng says that until just recently the networks wouldn't approve anything "that had ethnic situations in it. And nobody wants to put himself on the spit for trying to break the 'rules'."

Freleng had found out about the "rules" more than three decades earlier when his film credits read "I. Freleng," not

"Isidore Freleng." Freleng says, "Warner Brothers *suggested* [the change]. They didn't order it. They suggested it because down South at that time anything that's Jewish didn't go too well. We couldn't sell the show. They [the Southern distributors] said that the name is *out.* Warner Brothers said 'Why struggle with it?' So, we just used the initial *I.*" Later, it became a moot issue when Freleng decided that his credit should read *Friz Freleng,* reflecting his now-accepted Industry-wide nickname.[1]

For decades, representation of Blacks was universally excluded from cartoons, just as Blacks, with few exceptions, and then only cast in demeaning roles, were universally excluded from appearing in the movies, or even sitting with Whites who were watching the movies.

When Blacks were cast in animated cartoons, they were often portrayed in what, to audiences decades later, appeared to be racist caricatures. Some were less so than others. A couple of characters in the *Our Gang* cartoons, based upon the Hal Roach live-action theatrical shorts, were Black, but their roles were often incidental and the stereotypes muted.

Bosko, created by Hugh Harman and Rudy Ising, first appeared in *Sinking in the Bathtub*, released in May 1930. Bosko spoke a variety of Black English in the first film, but Standard English thereafter and could easily have been a White character if a few mannerisms had been deleted. Bosko starred in thirty-nine cartoons between 1930 and 1933. When Harman and Ising went to MGM in 1933, Bosko went with them, starring in an additional eight cartoons between 1933 and 1938.

The year Bosko went to MGM, Warner Brothers created Buddy, a WASPy kind of a kid, based upon Bosko, but not as successful. The series ended in 1935.

Nevertheless, because of the success of Bosko, other studios created their own Black characters. The Lantz Studio created Little Eight Ball, Warner Brothers created a one-shot character, Niccodemus; and George Pal created Jasper.

Harriet Beecher Stowe's *Uncle Tom's Cabin,* now regarded by media historians as the most influential novel in American literature, inspired numerous animated cartoons, all of them spoofs of the book, itself a not very realistic portrayal of Blacks. Paul Terry produced four *Uncle Tom* take-offs during the 1930s, none of them memorable. Tex Avery directed *Uncle Tom's Bungalow* in 1937 while at Warner Brothers, then followed it up nine years later at MGM with the popular *Uncle Tom's Cabana.*

Marc Connelly's *Green Pastures,* which received the Pulitzer Prize for the best drama of 1930, inspired animated cartoons featuring all-Black casts in heaven. In 1934, Friz Freleng directed, for Warner Brothers, *Going to Heaven on a Mule,* the story of a Black who enters the "swingin' gates ob Hebben," then is cast out after picking the forbidden fruit—a gin bottle from the forbidden tree. Three years later, using some of the animation from *Going to Heaven on a Mule,* Freleng directed the now-classic *Clean Pastures* with excellent musical production numbers and some "hep angels" (caricatures of Cab Calloway, Fats Waller, Louis Armstrong and the Mills Brothers) who go to Earth to lead the sinners out of the Hades, Inc. nightclub and into the path to heaven.

Jazz, a distinctively African-American musical form, was transformed into cartoons with reasonable accuracy, although the characters were often what audiences might later regard as stereotypes. During the late 1930s and early 1940s, Walter Lantz produced several all-Black cartoon musicals, including *Scrub Me Momma With a Boogie Beat* and *The Boogie Woogie Man.* The cartoons were well-directed and animated, and the music lively and appropriate, but are no longer shown in television syndication.

*Coal Black and the Sebben Dwarfs,* released by Warner Brothers in December 1942, is universally regarded by those in animation as one of the best cartoons ever produced. Directed by Bob Clampett, with story by Warren Foster and animation by Rod Scribner, the cartoon featured 'So White' in a hilarious fast-paced spoof of the Disney classic five years earlier. A few months later Clampett, Foster and Scribner produced *Tin Pan Alley Cats,* featuring a Fats Waller-like character on a "head trip." However, as times changed, and as people's attitudes began changing, both cartoons were left in the vaults, and have only recently become available.

*Amos 'n' Andy,* for several years the most popular radio

show in America, was transformed into animation in 1934 by the Van Beuren Studio. However, only two episodes were produced, both directed by George Stallings. Three decades later, Freeman Gosden and Charles Correll who had originated *Amos 'n' Andy* in 1928, and starred in both the radio show and the cartoons, reprised their roles in *Calvin and the Colonel* (1961-1962). Because of shifting values, and a different mass awareness of what were now regarded as stereotyped images of Blacks, Calvin (an Andy-figure) became a not-so-bright bear; the Colonel (the Kingfish), was a sly and crafty fox. However the language that both characters spoke was a muted variety of American Black English.

A Black character, a maid, appeared in the original version of Walt Disney's *Fantasia*, but was left in the archives when the film was re-released. In this case, however, it was because Disney executives may have realized that the character could have been offensive to some.

When MGM, and later Hanna-Barbera, began remaking Tom and Jerry cartoons for television, one of the continuing characters from the 1940s, Mammy Two-Shoes, a maid, was also retired.

Blacks seldom appear in television cartoons. However, one series that features Blacks, portraying them in realistic situations, is *Fat Albert*, written by Bill Danch, and produced by Bill Cosby, Norm Prescott and Lou Scheimer for Filmation studios. The series, which premiered in 1972, featured characters created by Cosby.

Three other series that featured Blacks were *The Harlem Globetrotters* (1970-1973, 1979-1980), produced by Hanna-Barbera; *The Jackson Five* (1971-1973), produced by Rankin-Bass; and *I'm the Greatest—The Adventures of Muhammad Ali* (1977), a Farmhouse Films production that survived only a half-season.

During World War II, a number of cartoons denigrated an entire race of people by portraying the Japanese in grotesquely stereotyped fashion. Most of the major cartoon characters had their encounters with Japanese soldiers—in 1943, Popeye defeated the Japanese in *You're a Sap, Mister Jap*; and in 1944, Bugs Bunny became the hero in *Nip the Nips*. However, one of the most racist—and most popular—cartoons was *Tokio-Jokio,* produced in 1943 by Warner Brothers. The focus of the cartoon—in essence, a series of blackouts—was not so much the defeat of the Japanese empire but to show the Japanese military as inept and foolish, and the Japanese people in the "Ah so!" caricature, complete with buck teeth and round glasses.

It wasn't until 1959 that an Oriental character was given favorable treatment on screen. Hashimoto, a Japanese house mouse with a command of judo and Japanese folklore, became the star of a series of fourteen cartoons during the next four years. Director of most of the episodes, including the first one, *Hashimoto-san,* was Bob Kuwahara. The cartoons were produced by Terrytoons.

*The Amazing Chan and the Chan Clan* (1972-1974), produced by Hanna-Barbera, was a parody of the many Charlie Chan movies. To be a parody, there must be some resemblance to the original. Therefore the leading character was named Chan. His children were named Henry, Stanley, Suzie, Alan, Anne, Tom, Flip, Nancy and Mimi. Interestingly, most of the voices were those of Chinese-surnamed individuals.

In the United States during World War I, anything that sounded German was forbidden. Sauerkraut, for instance, became Victory Cabbage; and thousands of persons Anglicized their German-sounding names.

One series that met an abrupt end was *The Katzenjammer Kids,* produced by Gregory LaCava, and based upon the highly-successful newspaper comic strip written and drawn by Rudolph Dirk, beginning in 1897. Between the end of 1916 and mid-1918, LaCava produced twenty-three animated shorts, completing the last cartoon four months before the Armistice. The series, retitled *The Captain and the Kids,* again went into production in 1938, but was terminated after fifteen shorts. The reason, however, had nothing to do with the mounting German terror that was unleashing another world war. According to Friz Freleng, who directed many of the shows, "I knew the Katzenjammer Kids wouldn't sell. They were humanoid characters. Humanoids were not selling. The animal pairs . . . were what was [selling]."[2]

During World War II, says Dick Huemer, who wrote *Dumbo* and a number of other Disney cartoons, "there was no conscious effort at any of the studios to eliminate German-sounding names." He explains, however, that certain names, such as Hans and Fritz, never came up.

Occasionally, if ethnic names are used, they are tagged onto jinxed characters. In an episode of *Bailey's Comets*, the jinx was an Arab named Ali Boo Boo. In a continuing role in Hanna-Barbera's *Pebbles and Bamm-Bamm* series, the jinx was Schleprock.

During the "Golden Age of Animation," when animals and animal combinations dominated the screen, other naming patterns prevailed. But in the television age more human characters emerged, leaving major naming problems for the Industry. The result was to take the "obvious way out," naming and creating characters after the dominant American sub-culture.

"Green; that's the color that sets the standards," says one veteran writer. "It's money. And money comes from advertisers. And advertisers are the businessmen with three-piece suits and Ivy League education. Maybe they're someone from the Bible Belt who developed a large business. The Jews may have been involved in the creative aspects of the Industry, but the WASPs are the advertisers."

Stephen R. Bosustow who produced educational films after having founded and guided UPA into Industry-wide importance, said, "The question of restrictions never came up. Had it been a slur, I wouldn't accept it. We thought about people, and we didn't have that kind of conflict. But, in general, we try to keep the naming of characters down the middle. That's just the way it is."

More blunt is the view of one of the former top executives at Hanna-Barbera. "Let's face it," he once said, "the medium itself is largely WASPish."

Actually, the medium, itself, is not largely WASPish. Nor are many of the Industry's most creative personnel WASPs. But the perception, however incorrect, remains. Studio personnel believe that viewers, and especially the advertisers with millions to invest, are more comfortable with persons

The Jetsons

"they" can identify with—usually, White, Anglo-Saxon, and Protestant.

In late 1982, it was revealed that all three major television networks used outside consultants to evaluate the "appropriateness" of project ideas for the networks. One of the major criteria was the race and religion of main characters—a minority lead character would cost the writer "points."

Hanna-Barbera's *The Flintstones*, which premiered on the ABC television network in the 1960-1961 season, was the first prime-time animated television series for adults as well as children. It was also a "safe" series—one based upon Jackie Gleason's highly successful *The Honeymooners*—but modified by being animated and set in the Stone Age. The lead characters in *The Honeymooners* were named Ralph and Alice; the lead characters in *The Flintstones* were named Fred and Wilma. The secondary characters in *The Honeymooners* were named Ed and Trixie; the secondary characters in *The Flintstones* were named Barney and Betty. Several seasons later, when the Flintstones and the Rubbles had children, character naming took a slight twist. Instead of WASP names, the Flintstones named their daughter "Pebbles" following a nationwide contest; the Rubbles named their son "Bamm-Bamm." The names were descriptive—Pebbles because she was smaller than a (flint) stone, and Bamm-Bamm because he was strong and carried a club which he banged with earthquake-like force.

Having achieved success with a *Honeymooners* spin-off into the past, Hanna-Barbera looked to the future. The result was *The Jetsons* (1963-1964), a Jackie Gleason *Honeymooners* set in the space age. Instead of two couples, there was one couple with two children. The parents were named George and Jane; the children were named Judy and Elroy. Their maid-robot was Rosie.

Other Hanna-Barbera human families in situation comedy format included the Holidays, the Boyles, the Carters, the Devlins and the Days. In *Roman Holidays* (1972-1973), a series set at the time of the glory of the Roman Empire—and long before Protestants or Catholics were anything to contend with—the leading characters were named Gus, Laurie, Happius, Precocia, Groovia, Herman and Henrietta, as well as

'Roman Holidays'

Evictus, the landlord; and Tyconnius, the businessman. Brutus, the pet lion, had the only name resembling Latin. As for Precocia? It wasn't until centuries after the decline of the Roman Empire that families began naming their children for desired characteristics—Faith, Hope, Charity and Precocia.

The Boyles, stars of *Wait Till Your Father Gets Home* (1972-1974), a contemporary comedy, were named Harry, Irma, Chet, Alice and Jamie. The super-patriotic neighbor was named Ralph. In *The Micro-Venture* (1973), a four-episode series, the leading characters were Prof. Carter and his children, Jill and Mike.

The Devlins, a family of orphans who entered the world of motorcycle racing, were led by older brother Ernie. Hank and Sandy were the other children; Todd was their best friend. There were only sixteen episodes of the show which premiered in 1974.

*These are the Days* (1974-1976), set about the time that mass production was changing the development of America, included Homer, Danny, Kathy, Ben and Martha.

In addition to a number of WASPish-named "biological" families, Hanna-Barbera also had a number of "sociological" families. Most of these sociological families were placed in a science-fiction setting. The leading characters of *The Adventures of Johnny Quest* (1964-1965) were Dr. Benton Quest; his son, Johnny; and researcher Roger Bannon. (Their East Indian companion, however, was named Hadji.) In *Sealab 2020* (1972-1973), the major characters were Mike Murphy, Paul Williams, Hal, Gail, Ed, Bobby, Jamie, Sallie and Mrs. Thomas. In *Danger Island*, the major characters were named Dr. Hayden, Leslie, Link and Morgan.

The major characters in *Here Come the Clowns* were named Julie, Max, Ernie, Sue, Mike, Adam and Tabitha. It was easy to identify the circus people—they weren't WASPs. Among the circus people were Hadji, Count Krumley, Muscles, Ducks, Boris, Hi-Rise and Ronko.

*Captain Caveman* (1979-1980) was based upon the live-action television show *Charlie's Angels*. The leader was Captain Caveman, but his "teen angels" were WASPy Taffy, Brenda and Dee Dee.

'Wait 'Til Your Father Gets Home'

In television animation, if one dog is successful, then several dogs are likely to be even more successful. At Hanna-Barbera there were many dogs. The first one was the anthropomorphized Huckleberry Hound who debuted in 1958. Following him were Scooby Doo, Scrappy Doo, Goober and Buford among many others, each of whom bore some faint resemblance to Pluto, created by Walt Disney in 1930. However, each of the Hanna-Barbera dogs had WASP-human companions. The human companions of Scooby Doo, one of Hanna-Barbera's most popular creations, were Freddy, Daphne, Shaggy and Velma. The human companions for Goober, a Scooby-like dog who had a two-year run, beginning in 1973, plus re-runs, were Ted, Tina and Gillie. For southern country dog Buford, Woody and Cindy Mae provided companionship during the 1979-1980 season.

After surveying the entire rock scene, a number of leading cartoon producers decided in the late 1970s that it would be profitable if they too had some rock groups in animated form. Soon, rock groups became almost as prolific as animated animals or human families. In addition to animated versions of the Beatles, there were Hanna-Barbera's *Josie and the Pussycats, Butch Cassidy and the Sundance Kids* and *The Partridge Family*. The major characters in *Josie and the Pussycats* (1970-1974), which was later revamped, given a new format and sent into outer space, were Josie, Alexandra, Valerie, Alex, Melody and Alan. *The Partridge Family* (1974-1975), based on the live-action television series, was also sent into animated outer space; they were named Keith, Danny, Lori, Chris, Tracy and Shirley. Even the "new" characters, the ones from outer space, had WASPy-sounding names—Veenie, Marian Moonglow and Orbit. The young people in *Butch Cassidy and the Sundance Kids* (1973-1974) were Merilee, Harvey and Steffy. The leader of the group was, naturally, Butch Cassidy who took his name from the real-life outlaw who was popularized by the Robert Redford-Paul Newman movie.

Also from Hanna-Barbera came *The Fantastic Four* (1967-1970), four persons with individual superhuman abilities and WASP names—Reed, Sue, Johnny and Ben. The fantastic four, who originated in Marvel Comics, were modified in 1978 when DePatie-Freleng took over the animation. Johnny Storm, the human torch, was extinguished, replaced by Herbie the Robot.

Another "four" the gang of *Emergency Plus 4* (1973-1976), was based on the live-action show, *Emergency*. *Emergency Plus 4*, produced by Fred Calvert Productions, featured characters from the original show, firefighter-paramedics Roy DeSoto and John Gage (portrayed by Kevin Tighe and Randolph Mantooth in both series), as well as four young helpers—Sally, Matt, Jason and Randy.

Will WASP names continue to dominate the names for leading characters in the 1980s? It's hard to tell, but it is possible to predict that when advertisers begin using more ethnic situations, with non-WASP characters with non-WASP names, then the cartoon series won't be far behind.

*Valley of the Dinosaurs*

# 11/ The Primitive Past and the Distant Future

With the possible exception of *The Flintstones*, the present transported to the past; *The Jetsons,* the present transported into the future; and animated series based upon other live-action comedies, many television cartoon series with time frames other than the present are remarkably similar. The plots and characters are alike; the naming patterns are alike. Most names, whether primitive past or distant future, have the same essential onomastic elements.

In Hanna-Barbera's *Valley of the Dinosaurs*, which premiered in the 1974-1975 season, a modern-day family found itself trapped in a primitive valley; their only companions were a Neanderthal family. The main characters from the present, all with WASP names, were John, Kim, Katie and Greg; the Neanderthal family names were Gorok, Gara, Lik and Tana. In *Dino Boy*, a short-lived series about a young man and a caveman, the main characters were Dino and Ugh. Another Hanna-Barbera caveman was Captain Caveman, a one-season spin-off of *Charlie's Angels.*

In *Mighty Mightor* (1967-1969), a mythological set of stories that could either be viewed as past or future, depending on one's perspective, the main characters were Mightor (also known as Tor), Sheera, Pondo, L'il Rok, Ork and Tog. For *Herculoids* (1967-1969), a futuristic series, the main characters were Zandor, Tarra (perhaps based upon the mansion in *Gone With the Wind*), Dorno, Zok, Gloop, Gleep and Igoo. In *Thundarr, the Barbarian* (1981-1982), another series set in the future—two thousand years after a runaway planet caused the destruction of Earth in 1994—civilization had begun to rebuild itself, but was still barbaric, though cosmic mutations had caused supernatural powers to develop. The descriptively-named Thundarr, a hero not too unlike Mightor or Zandor,

157

helped bring about the rebirth of civilization. For the animated version of *Lost in Space*, Hanna-Barbera added Lar, Kal and Brack, residents of Throg, to the characters from the live-action television show.

The title character of Hanna-Barbera's *Korg—70,000 B.C.*, which had a short run beginning in the 1974-1975 season, underwent several name changes before *the* name was selected. Although *Korg* was live-action, the naming process was similar to the way Hanna-Barbera handled its animated shows. The original name of Korg was Gan-lo. According to one former Hanna-Barbera executive, Gan-lo was too long, so the name was recast as Dorek. Dorek led to Krog and Krog was transformed as Korg. "We couldn't use Krog," he says, "because it sounded too much like Grog, a character in the *B.C.* comic strip." The character Bok was originally Pol, but the studio "didn't like the sound of Pol." The other characters were named Mara, Tane, Tor and Ree.

Hanna-Barbera writers, perhaps subconsciously, place a heavy emphasis on the velar stops—the *g* and *k* sounds— because "they sound primitive." Actually, there is no evidence, linguistic or otherwise, to suggest such a conclusion. But, perception of reality, in animation as in real-life, often determines what will be used and what "works." Soon, the perception becomes embedded as reality in the minds of the audience.

Ask any six-year-old TV viewer what name sounds more "time foreign," Jimmy or Kirk, and it's possible, with all the *g* and *k* sounds floating around past-and-future TV shows, that the kid picks out Kirk.

# Epilogue

The study of the evolution of animation naming practices is the study of the names of modern folk heroes. Children growing up in the 1980s are better versed in the escapades of the characters who appear on Saturday and Sunday morning television than they are in the lives of the great characters of literature. But, if children do not read as much today as they did three or four decades ago, we shouldn't turn to television for our wrath, for our excuses, for there are enough hours in every day for children not only to watch their favorite heroes, but also to read, if they wish to do so.

Perhaps, for those in the elementary grades, it isn't even an evil trade-off, trading some literary heroes for some animated ones. And, certainly, the best animated cartoons will always be as important, and enjoyable, perhaps as meaningful, as some of the better children's stories.

The cartoon hero, animated and placed into the electronic mass medium known as television, is today's folk hero to the young. It is also society's statement about itself.

# Notes

## CHAPTER 1

[1]Silverman later became vice-president of programming for CBS-TV, president of ABC Entertainment, and president of NBC.

[2]By the late 1970s, the networks began their Saturday cartoon programming as early as 7 a.m. Some network-affiliated stations began airing cartoons as early as 6 a.m.

[3]Quoted in "TV's Saturday Gold Mine," *Business Week*, August 2, 1969, p. 96.

[4]A cel (from "celluloid") is a clear, transparent overlay onto which animators draw parts of a character or the entire character. The cel is then placed against other cels which are placed against backgrounds. The entire set is then photographed.

## CHAPTER 2

[1]Oswald was distributed by the Mintz Co., then became a Walter Lantz character.

[2]Although all Felix cartoons included the screen credit, "by Pat Sullivan," and although Sullivan as studio head promoted Felix, it is now acknowledged that it was Messmer who created and animated the black cat. It was common for a studio to take the identity for the creation of a character, the reasoning being that it was a team effort that produced the character.

[3]Quoted in "Otto Messmer," by John Canemaker, *Millimeter*, September 1976, p. 58.

[4]Diane Disney Miller, "The Mouse That Roared," *Saturday Evening Post*, July/August 1977, p. 50.

[5]Anonymous, *The Adventures of Mickey Mouse*, David McKay (Philadelphia, 1931), p. 1.

## CHAPTER 4

[1]Both the voice and characterization of Huckleberry Hound were those of three characters who first appeared in Tex Avery cartoons—*The Three Little Pups* (1953, MGM); *Billy Boy* (1954, MGM); and *I'm Cold* (1955, Walter Lantz). Later, Daws Butler did the voice for Huckleberry. The actual physical characteristics of Huckleberry Hound were created at the Hanna-Barbera studios. *Huckleberry Hound* became the first television cartoon to be produced by computer-aided animation.

## CHAPTER 5

[1]See *Walt Disney: The Art of Animation*, by Bob Thomas (Simon & Schuster, New York, 1958), p. 50.

[2]Most of the stories for the Droopy cartoons were written by Heck Allen, Avery's storyman at MGM for twelve years. Later, Allen wrote several outstanding Westerns, including *McKenna's Gold*. Animators with Avery during his years at MGM were Ray Abrams, Preston Blair, Irven Spence, Ed Love, Walt Clinton, Louis Schmitt, William Shull, Grant Simmons, Bob Cannon and Michael Lah. Scott Bradley was music director.

*161*

**Chapter 6.**

[1]During World War II, the U.S. Navy nicknamed the PBY, an amphibious airplane, "The Flying Dumbo."

[2]Freleng had hired a real stutterer to make the voice sound natural, but two years later when the actor left Warner Brothers, Mel Blanc was hired. Blanc became the voices for most of the Warner Brothers characters.

[3]Quoted in *Tex Avery: King of the Cartoons*, by Joe Adamson (Popular Library, New York, 1975), pp. 162-163.

[4]*Ibid.*

[5]Avery also directed Bugs Bunny in *The Heckling Hare* and *All This and Rabbit Stew*, both released in 1941.

[6]See *The Fleischer Story*, by Leslie Cabarga (Nostalgia Press, New York, 1976), p. 133.

[7]Betty Boop cartoons were discontinued in 1939 when the Fleischers moved their studios to Miami.

[8]I. Klein, "Mighty Mouse," *Cartoonists Pro-Files*, December 1973, p. 23.

**CHAPTER 7**

[1]The Fleischer Studio animated the original Popeye cartoons; in the 1980s, Hanna-Barbera created its form of Popeye.

[2]The name Sody Quacker was both a pun and an inside joke—Bob Clampett's wife is named Sody.

**CHAPTER 8**

[1]"The Sorcerer's Apprentice" segment starred Mickey Mouse in what was planned as his triumphant return to stardom after slipping in popularity. But Mickey was cast as an actor playing a role.

[2]Quoted in *Vlad Tytla: Animation's Michaelangelo,"* by John Canemaker, *Cinefantastique, Fall* 1976.

[3]Several scenes were cut from *Red Hot Riding Hood* when censors from the Hays Office found them "too suggestive."

**CHAPTER 9**

[1]Freleng got his nickname from pioneer cartoon producer Hugh Harman. Freleng explains that Harman was a devoted reader of a cartoon character, Congressman Frisby. "At first," says Freleng, "I was called Congressman Frisby, then Congressman, and Frizby, then finally Friz."

[2]Quoted in *The Encyclopedia of Animated Cartoon Series,* by Jeff Lenburg (Arlington House, Westport, Ct., 1981), p. 30.

# Selected Bibliography

Adamakos, Peter, "Ub Iwerks," *Mindrot*, No. 7 (June 1977).

Adamson, Joe, "Chuck Jones Interviewed," in *The American Animated Cartoon*, written by Gerald Peary and Danny Peary (E.P. Dutton, New York, 1980).

—————,"Joe Adamson Talks with Richard Huemer," *AFI Report*, Vol. 5, No. 2 (Summer 1974), pp. 10-17.

—————, *Tex Avery: King of the Cartoons* (Popular Library, New York, 1975).

—————, "Working for the Fleischers: An Interview with Dick Huemer," *Funnyworld*, No. 16 (Winter 1974-1975), pp. 23-28, 124.

Alpert, Hollis, "Manic World of Ralph Bakshi," *Saturday Review World*, Vol. 1 (March 9, 1974), pp. 40-41, 56.

Bain, David, Bruce Harris, *Mickey Mouse: Fifty Happy Years* (Harmony House, New York, 1977).

Barrier, Mike, "The Black Cauldron—Disney's Production for 1984," *Funnyworld*, No. 20 (Summer 1979), pp. 27-31.

—————, "Building a Better Mousetrap—Fifty Years of Disney Animation, *Funnyworld*, No. 20 (Summer 1979), pp. 6-22.

—————, "Of Mice, Wabbits, Ducks and Men," *AFI Report*, Vol. 5, No. 2 (Summer 1974), pp. 18-26.

Beckerman, Howard, "Whatever Happened to Ernest Pintoff?" *Filmmakers Newsletter,* Vol. 7, No. 3 (January 1974).

Beke, Gregory, "Ralph Bakshi," *Millimeter*, Vol. 3, No. 4 (April 1975), pp. 18-19.

Bertino, Tom, "Hugh Harman and Rudolph Ising at Warner Brothers," *Mindrot*, No. 5 (December 1976).

—————, "Taking the Boop Out of Betty," *Mindrot, No XX* (October 1977).

Bogdanovich, Peter, "Hollywood," *Esquire*, Vol. 77, No. 3 (March 1972), pp. 66, 73-74.

Bray, J. "Development of Animated Cartoons," *Moving Picture World*, No. 33 (July 21, 1917), pp. 395-398.

Brown, Harry, "Road Runner and Wile E. Coyote," *Close-Ups: The Movie Star Book*, edited by Danny Peary (Workman Publishing Co., New York, 1978).

Cabarga, Leslie, *The Fleischer Story* (Nostalgia Press, New York, 1977).

Canemaker, John, "A Day with J.R. Bray," *Yearbook*, the International Animated Film Society (ASIFA-West, Los Angeles, 1975).

—————, *Animated Raggedy Ann and Andy, The; An Intimate Look at the Art of Animation, Its History, Techniques and Artists,* Bobbs-Merrill Co., Indianapolis, 1977.)

—————, "Animation History and Shamus Culhane," *Filmmaker's Newsletter*, Vol. 7, No. 8 (June 1974), pp. 23-28.

—————, "Animation Renaissance," *Horizon*, Vol. 23 (March 1980), pp. 44-53.

—————, "Animation Today," *Millimeter*, Vol. 5, No. 9 (October 1977), pp. 50-52, 55.

—————, "Art Babbitt: The Animator as Firebrand," *Millimeter*, Vol. 3, No. 9 (September 1975), pp. 8-10, 12, 42-44.

—————, "Birth of Animation, The," *Millimeter*, Vol. 3, No. 4 (April

1975), pp. 14-16.

————, "Disney Design, 1928-1979," *Millimeter*, Vol. 7, No. 2 (February 1979), pp. 102-109.

————, "Grim Natwick," *Film Comment*, Vol. 11, No. 1 (January—February 1975), pp. 57-61.

————, "Otto Messmer and Felix the Cat," *Millimeter*, Vol. 4, No. 9 (September 1976), pp. 32-34, 58-61.

————, "Profile of a Living Animation Legend: J.R. Bray," *Filmmakers Newsletter*, Vol. 8, No. 3 (January 1975), pp. 28-31.

————, "Winsor McCay," *Film Comment*, Vol. 11, No. 1 (January February, 1975), pp. 44-47.

"Cheaper Cartoons," *Business Week*, No. 1444 (May 4, 1957), pp. 192-194.

Cocks, Jay "World Jones Made, The," *Time*, Vol. 102 (December 17, 1973), p. 76.

Crafton, Don, *Before Mickey* (MIT Press, Cambridge, Mass, 1982).

Crowther, Bosley, "McBoing-Boing, Magoo and Bosustow," *The New York Times Magazine*, Vol. 102 (December 21, 1952), pp. 14-15, 23.

Culhane, John, "Mouse for All Seasons," *Saturday Review*, Vol. 5, (November 1978), pp. 50-51.

De Mille, William, "Mickey *versus* Popeye," *The Forum*, Vol. 94, No. 5 (November 1935), pp. 295-297.

DeRoos, Robert, "Magic Worlds of Walt Disney," *National Geographic Magazine*, Vol. 124, No. 8 (August 1963), pp. 158-207.

Disney Productions, *Magic Moments*, A. Mondadori Editions (Milan, Italy, 1973).

Disney, Walt, "How I Cartooned Alice," *Films in Review*, Vol. 2 (February 1961), pp. 7-11.

————, "Life Story of Mickey Mouse, The" *Windsor Magazine*, Vol. 79, No. 469 (January 1934), pp. 259-263.

————, "Mickey Mouse—How He Was Born," *Windsor Magazine*, Vol. 74, (October 1931), pp. 641-645.

Edera, Bruno, *Full-Length Animated Feature Films* (Hastings House, New York, 1977).

Finch, Christopher, *The Art of Walt Disney*, Harry N. Abrams, (New York) 1973.

Friedwald, Will, and Herry Beck, *The Warner Brothers' Cartoons Scarecrow Press*, (Metuchen, N.J.), 1981.

Geis, Darlene, ed., *Walt Disney's Treasurey of Stories from Silly Symphonies* (Abrams, (New York), 1981.

Gianeri, Enrico, *Storia del Cartone Annato*, Editrice Omnia (Milan, Italy), 1960.

Gillam, Terry and Lucinda Cowell, *Animations of Mortality*, Methuen, (London), 1979.

Glut, Donald F. and Jim Harmon, *The Great Television Heroes*, Doubleday, (Garden City, N.Y.), 1975.

Hearn, Michael Patrick, "Animated Art of Winsor McCay," *American Artist*, Vol. 39, No. 394 (May 1975), pp. 28-33.

Heraldson, Donald, *Creators of Life: A History of Animation*, Drake Publishers (New York), 1975.

Hoffer, Tom W., "From Comic Strips to Animation: Some Perspective on Winsor McCay," *The Journal of the University Film Association*, Vol. 28, No. 2 (Spring 1976), pp. 23-32.

Horn, Maurice, ed., *The World Encyclopedia of Cartoon* (Gale, Detroit, 1980).

Horrigan, William, "Just About Crazy," in *The American Animated Cartoon,"* edited by Gerald Peary and Danny Peary, Dutton (New York) 1980, pp. 37-42.

Hubley, John, "Beyond Pigs and Bunnies: The New Animator's Art," *American Scholar,* Vol. 44, No. 2 (Spring 1975), pp. 213-223.

Hullet, S., "Star is Drawn," *Film Comment,* Vol. 15 (January 1979), pp. 13-15.

Johnston, A., "Will The Next Mr. Disney Please Stand Up . . . ?" *MacLeans,* Vol. 95 (April 28, 1980), pp. 52.

Johnston, Claire and Paul Williams, *Frank Tashlin,* Edinburg Film Festival (Edinburgh, Scotland), 1971.

Jones, Chuck, "Animation is a Gift Word," *AFI Report,* Vol. 5, No. 2 (Summer 1974), pp. 27-29.

————, "Friz Freleng," *Millimeter,* Vol. 4, No. 11 (November 1976), pp. 20-22, 24.

Klein, I. "I. Klein Story, The," *I.A.T.S.E. Official Bulletin,* No. 456, (Autumn 1967), pp. 34-35.

————, "Mighty Mouse," *Cartoonists Pro-files,* Vol. 1, No. 20 (December 1973), pp. 21-23.

————, "Screen Gems Made of Paste—Memories of the Charles Mintz Studio," *Funnyworld,* No. 20 (Summer 1979), pp. 39-41.

Lamour, Philippe, "The New Art: Mickey Mouse—A Note on the Talking Film," *New Hope,* Vol. 2, No. 5 (September 15, 1934), pp. 9, 15.

Langer, Mark, "Max and Dave Fleischer," *Film Comment,* Vol. 11, No. 1 (January-February 1975), pp. 44-56.

Lutz, George Edwin, *Animated Cartoons; How They are Made, Their Origin and Design* (Charles Scribner's, New York, 1926).

Maltin, Leonard, *Disney Films, The.* (Crown Publishers, (New York 1973).

————, *Of Mice and Rabbits,* New American Library, (New York), 1980.

————, "Popeye," *Film Fan Monthly* No. 144 (June 1973), pp. 3-21.

MacDonald, Dwight, "Complete Works of Ernest Pintoff," *Esquire,* Vol. 61, No. 4 (April 1964), pp. 16, 18.

Macek, Carl and Susan Cohn, *The Art of 'Heavy Metal': Animation for the Eighties,* New York Zoetrope, (New York), 1981.

Martarella, Frank David, "Animated Cinema," *America,* Vol. 120, No. 10 (March 8, 1969), pp. 271-273.

McCay, Winsor, "Movie Cartoons," *Cartoon and Movie Magazine,* Vol. XX, No. 31 (April 1927), pp.xxx.

McGilligan, Patrick, "Robert Clampett," in *The American Animated Cartoon,* edited by Gerald Peary and Danny Peary, Dutton (New York), 1980, pp. 150-157.

Miller, Diane Disney, "The Mouse that Roared," *The Saturday Evening Post,* Vol. 249, No 4 (July 3, 1977), p. 50.

————. *The Story of Walt Disney,* as told to Pete Martin, Holt (New York), 1956.

Mishkin, Lee, "Musings of an Expatriate," *AFI Report,* Vol. 5, No. 2 (Summer 1974), pp. 30-32.

Mouse, Mickey, "The Mouse Mimes the Masters," *The Saturday Evening Post,* Vol. 250, No. 8 (November 1978), pp. 82-83.

"Mousetrap," *Newsweek,* Vol. 52, No. xxx (July 7, 1958), p. 72.

Nardone, Mark, "Robert McKimson Interviewed," in *The American Animated Cartoon,* edited by Gerald Peary and Danny Peary Dutton, (New York), 1980, pp. 142-149.

—————, "Saturday Morning Cartoons," in *TV Book*, edited by Judy Fireman (Workman Publishing, New York, 1977).

Olshan, Mike, "Animation Grows Up," *Millimeter,* Vol. 2, No. 9 (September 1974), pp. 28-29, 46-47.

—————, "Interview with Ralph Bakshi," *Millimeter,* Vol. 2, No. 9 (September 1974), pp. 28-29, 46-47.

O'Sullivan, Judith, "In Search of Winsor McCay," *AFI Report*, Vol. 5, No. 2 (Summer 1974), pp. 3-9.

Peary, Gerald and Danny Peary, *The American Animated Cartoon: A Critical Anthology,* Dutton, (New York), 1980.

"Put a Panther in Your Tank," *Time*, Vol. 86, No. 14 (October 1, 1965), p. 90.

"Return of the Animals," *Newsweek,* Vol. 57, (May 22, 1961).

Rider, David (compiler), *The Great Cartoon Movie Parade,* Bounty Books (New York), 1976.

Scanlon, P., "Animated Man: Ralph Bakshi," *Rolling Stone,* No. 283 (January 25, 1979), pp. 28, 30-32.

Scheib, Ronnie, "Tex Arcana: The Cartoons of Tex Avery," in *The American Animated Cartoon,* edited by Gerald Peary and Danny Peary (Dutton, New York, 1980), pp. 110-127.

Schickel, Richard, *The Disney Version* (Simon & Schuster, New York, 1968).

—————, "Magnificent Obsessives," *Time,* Vol. 114, No. 17 (October 22, 1979), pp. 88, 90.

Seldes, Gilbert, "Walt Disney," *The New Yorker,* Vol. 7, No. 44 (December 19, 1931), pp. 23-27.

Shalit, Gene, "Gene Slips Us a Mickey," *Ladies Home Journal*, Vol. 94, No. 12 (December 1977), pp. 8, 10.

Slafer, Eugene, "A Conversation With Bill Hanna," in *The American Animated Cartoon*, edited by Gerald Peary and Danny Peary (Dutton, New York, 1980), pp. 255-260.

Smith, Conrad, "The Early History of Animation," *The Journal of the University Film Association,* Vol. 29, No. 3 (Summer 1977), pp. 23-30.

Smith, David, "Ben Sharpsteen," *Millimeter,* Vol. 3, No. 4 (April 1975), pp. 38-40, 42, 44-45.

—————, "Ub Iwerks," *Funnyworld,* No. 14 (Spring 1972), pp. 32-37, 47.

Solomon, Charles, "Fantastic Voyage," *Crawdaddy,* No. 90 (November 1978), pp. 57-60.

"Stars and B'ars," *Time,* Vol. 83, No. 24 (June 12, 1964), pp. 109, 112.

Stephenson, Ralph, *The Animated Film* Tantivy Press, (London), 1973.

—————, *Action in the Cinema,* A. Zwemmer (London), 1967.

Steward, Jon, "Fritz the Cat," *Ramparts,* Vol. 10, No. 3 (March 1972), pp. 43-48.

Stocker, Joseph, "Magnificent Magoo," *American Mercury* (Vol. 86, No. 411 (April 1958), pp. 129-133.

Sullivan, Catherine, "United Productions of America," *American Artist,* Vol. 19 (November 1955), pp. 34-39, 63-64.

Taylor, Deems, *Walt Disney's Fantasia* (Simon & Schuster, New York, 1940).

Thiesen, Earl, "The History of the Animated Cartoon," *Journal of the Society of Motion Picture Engineers,* Vol. 21, No. 3 (September 1933), pp. 239-249.

————, *Walt Disney: An American Original* (Simon & Schuster, New York, 1976).

————, *Walt Disney: Magician of the Movies* (Grosset & Dunlap, New York, 1966).

Thomas, Frank and Ollie Johnston, *Disney Animation: The Illusion of Life,* Abbeville Press (New York), 1981.

Thompson, Richard, "Meep-Meep!" *Film Comment,* Vol. 12, No. 3 (May-June 1976), pp. 37-39, 42-43.

"Up From Bugs," *The New Yorker,* Vol. 37, (August 5, 1961), p. 18.

Varlejs, Jana, "Cine-opsis," *Wilson Library Bulletin,* Vol. 50, No. 7 (March 1976), pp. 546-547.

Waller, Gregory A., "Mickey, Walt and Film Criticism from *Steamboat Willie* to *Bambi,*" in *The American Animated Cartoon,* edited by Gerald Peary and Danny Peary, Dutton, (New York), 1980, pp. 49-57.

Wealer, Gerald, "Tiggers Don't Like Honey," *Reporter,* Vol. 34, No. 8 (April 21, 1966), pp. 46-47.

Weinberg, Gretchen, "Interview with Ernest Pintoff," *Film Culture,* No. 31 (Winter 1963).

"Wizards," *Newsweek,* Vol. 89, (May 9, 1977, pp. 110, 112.

THIS IS THE NORMAL POSTURE OF DONALD'S BODY, AVOID OPPOSITE BEND

HAT USUALLY WORN AT A COCKY ANGLE

EYES WELL TO SIDES OF HEAD

NARROW RIDGE—NOT BUMP—ON END OF BILL

BILL BROAD & FLAT AT END

NECK WIDENS AT TOP

SHORT STOCKY ARMS

SHORT THICK LEGS ATTACHED WELL AT SIDES OF BODY

BILL LENGTH IS ¾ DIAM. OF HEAD

BRIDGE OF BILL ½ UP ON HEAD

PIT OF NECK

TOP OF FANNY

LEGS ATTACH

FEET WIDE APART, BLUNT TOES, MIDDLE ONE LONGEST

NOTE: BILL STILL FLAT IN THIS VIEW

THE TAIL IS A SIMPLE MASS OF FEATHERS BUILT ON A SMALL BUMP OF FLESH

FLAT FEELING TO TOP OF FANNY

TOP PART OF HAT APP. WIDTH OF HEAD

UPPER NECK ATTACHES TOWARD BACK OF HEAD—BASE OF SKULL ⅓ UP

IN THIS POSITION DON IS 3½ HEADS HIGH — OTHER POSITIONS VARY GREATLY

FEET ATTACH ⅔'s BACK ON FOOT

COMPARATIVE SIZES

59-342

# Index

*169*

©Hanna Barbera Productions, Inc.